CREATIVE WINEMAKING

by

André de Chambeau

WWWWW/Information Services, Inc.
Rochester, N.Y. 14609

CREATIVE WINEMAKING

Published by
WWWWW/Information Services, Inc.
Rochester, N.Y. 14609

Publisher: Robert A. Fowler
Executive Editor: Dennis G. Ruggeri
Managing Editor: Mrs. Oman Brunson

Contents

Part One:

Background Information

1. Winemaking As a Hobby—Welcome to one of today's most exciting hobbies—home winemaking. Home winemaking has all the elements of suspense, surprise and action. For centuries, it was essentially an art, with success depending on a combination of "good luck" and secret family recipes which were handed down from one generation to the next. Today this situation has changed and, while winemaking continues to be an art, modern science and technology have come to the home winemaker's aid. Now, it is both an art and a science. The modern winemaking hobbyist can make wine as good or better than many of the common commercial brands.

The hobby of winemaking itself has enjoyed phenomenal growth in modern times. Yet, you ask, "Why would anyone want to make their own wine?" There are a variety of answers. Some hobbyists would answer, to save money. But, by far and away, the majority would say they just enjoy making their very own wine.

As one hobbyist has put it, "Actually, I get a great deal of personal satisfaction from controlling a complex process to produce something of genuine value. I enjoy 'doing my own thing.' And, in this day and age of instant breakfasts and premixed Chinese foods, all the art has disappeared from most cooking. Yet, you can run the full gamut in winemaking. It can provide more variety than just about anything else. You can use the juice of grapes or cherries, or blackberries, and once in a while, 'let it all hang out' by mixing a concoction of dandelions, Karo syrup, food coloring and oregano.

"My wife thinks my wines are superb. Furthermore, I'll let you in on a little secret, my dinner guests are never bored. They often tell us, we make dining a real adventure since they never know what new brew we are going to serve. My wife and I feel this is a key to a stimulating evening, since my wines can turn the simplest meal into a memorable occasion. It brings new pleasures to entertaining.

"The great thing about winemaking is, you never know it all. You never have all the answers. There is always more to learn. You could safely say, it's a continuing thirst for knowledge."

As a winemaker, there are many options open to you. You can have the very pleasurable experience of growing your own fruit, or if you find this rather difficult since your apartment overlooks New York's 7th Avenue and 71st Street, you can purchase ripe fruit or concentrate to make your brew.

As a winemaker, there are two possible courses of action that are open to you. The first course allows you to utilize semi-professional winemaking equipment already commercially available. Here, you won't have all the equipment and facilities of a real winery, but you will have the next best thing to it, although on a very modest scale. This is what may be called a semi-professional approach. The second course of action is a somewhat helter-skelter method. You use some professional winemaking equipment, but you also improvise when the occasion arises. For simplification, we'll call this a "make-do" approach to winemaking.

Wine can be made from fruits, vegetables and even flowers. Fruits are the overwhelming favorite and are used to make the majority of wines.

Within the fruit category, grapes win hands down as they are used to make the very popular red and white wines, champagnes as well as sherries and vermouth. In fact, a great many true wine connoisseurs take the un-impeachable position that grape wine is the only wine and that wine made from any other juice is not truly a wine, but something less desirable.

Fruits other than grapes that can be made into wine include apples, cherries, plums, peaches, oranges, grape-fruits, blueberries, elderberries, raisins, cranberries and strawberries. These fruits can be fresh or in dried form.

Edible vegetables can also be made into wine. Al-though we are the first to admit that not all vegetables will result in inviting beverages, these wines are a great deal of fun to make and offer a wealth of winemaking knowledge. Satisfactory results have been achieved with beets, melons, celery, parsnips, tomatoes and even turnips!

Flowers by themselves cannot make wine, but their scents, colors and flavors can be captured by fermenting the blossoms in a sugar solution. Favorites are dande-lions, marigolds, clover, roses and violets. You might discover a few we missed!

2. Types of Wine—There are primarily five types of wines. The first type is the *appetizer* or *aperitif* wine that is ordinarily served before meals. Two favorites are the very popular sherry and vermouth. Many home wine connoisseurs serve sherry instead of the hackneyed man-hattan or martini cocktails. Serving sherry is very much in tune with the times as today's preference in alcoholic drinks is more and more toward lightness and flavor. Sherry is both. Many hosts would much prefer to serve their dinner guests a sherry rather than a martini be-cause all present will enjoy their dinner to a much fuller extent. Not only will all of their guests' senses be less dulled, but sherry will actually "whet their appetite" and help develop a keenness of taste for the forthcoming din-ner. In addition, sherry has always been a luncheon mainstay. The Plaza Hotel's cocktail lounge is daily invaded by the fair sex who offer living proof of the perpetual popularity of sherry. Sherry is not only ideal for sipping, but serves as a catalyst for very stimulating conversation.

Sweet and dry vermouths could also be classified as aperitifs, but their popularity ranks far beneath that of sherry. Generally, vermouth is combined with something else. If there were such an organization as the Vermouth Association, we imagine they would face a rather uphill battle in getting the average patron of the Plaza's Oak Room Bar to switch his favorite phrase from—"A dry 'mart' on the rocks. You call this dry!" to an expression of "heavy on the Cinzano and light on the Tangueray, s'il vous plait, Charles!" This is rather wishful thinking and vermouth as a drink, by itself, will continue to remain far down the popularity ladder.

A second type of wine is the ever popular and classic *red dinner wine*. Undoubtedly, you will want to make this wine yourself. When one thinks of red wine, the lovely vision of a beautiful raven-haired lass, like Sophia, comes to mind—gaily tromping grapes barefoot in a tub. As one enthusiastic and perhaps emotional (emotion and wine are synonymous) wine hobbyist told us, "there is something uniquely satisfying in making the red fluid burst forth by barefoot stomping in a tub!" and then when you throw in Sophia, you have all the ingredients—suspense, surprise and action. Actually, all this stomping is quite acceptable and practical in making red wine because the skins and juice are both used in primary fermentation. The skins provide the deep claret red color that typifies an attractive and very delicious red wine.

Red wines are generally served with beef or with those Italian delicacies such as spaghetti or lasagna. A general rule is—the heavier the food, the more robust the wine. This helps to account for the immense popularity of Italian food and red wine.

The third category of wine is *white table wine* which is also served with dinner. These wines may also be light or full bodied. The major difference between making white and red wine is that the skin is not used in making white wine. The grape that is ideally suited to making white wine has a skin that tends to slip off easily, while the skin of the red wine grape tends to cling tenaciously.

White wines should be served with light foods. Seafood dishes and white wine complement each other nicely. In addition, white wine will enhance the flavor of chicken, lamb, veal, and ham.

Rosé wines are the first cousins to the white wines. They are fast becoming one of the most popular of the homemade wines. The color of rosés can range from a rosy tint to darker pinks. They can be served with a great variety of foods and are especially appetizing with cold foods.

Another close relative to white wines is the flower wines. Flower wines have attracted the fancy of a great many home winemakers, as flowers add a fragrance and flavor to the wines that is at least truly unique. Home winemakers will blanch the petals of roses, dandelions and marigolds to produce the rich subtleties of flavor characteristic of these very special wines.

The fourth class of wines are the full-bodied, usually sweet wines that are served with *dessert* or as an *after-dinner* drink. Possible entries here include Port or Madeira and many of the fruit wines such as strawberry and raspberry. Quite frequently, brandy is added to these dessert wines to bring the alcohol content to 20%.

The last category is the *sparkling wines*. These wines may be white, pink, or red, and are commonly known as champagne, Cold Duck, and Sparkling Burgundy. Many of you will undoubtedly want to make these enchanting beverages. There can be no finer way to enliven a New Year's Eve party or your daughter's finest hour while, at the same time, conserving expense than by serving your own vintage bubbly.

3. Background of Grapes—The most important step in winemaking is selecting the grape. If the grapes are right, superior wines can be made. If the grapes are inferior, the wine will be no better than "vin ordinaire." The best method of ensuring good grapes is to grow your own and, for a small investment in time and money, you can. Grapes can be grown just about anywhere —from rocky hillsides to small backyard plots. The grapevines are available from specialized nurseries and distributors of winemaking equipment. These vines are generally two years old and, within two years after planting, should bear about 10 pounds of grapes yielding about a gallon of wine. These vines generally cost about $2.00 each, and they should be planted about 8 feet apart. Since you are permitted to make 200 gallons of wine each year, the 200 vines needed to make 200 gallons of wine require approximately 12,000 square feet or a ¼ acre of land. An investment in vines may be very attractive.

There are varieties of grapes that will grow in almost every part of the United States. If you are fortunate enough to live in the Napa Valley of California or in the Finger Lakes region of New York State, you can choose from a broad array of excellent grapes. There are numerous varieties that can be grown in your own backyard. Many of the New York State grapes have Indian names such as Catawbas, Delawares, Niagaras and Elviras. It is the juice from these same grapes that make the world renowned New York State champagnes. A little further west of the Finger Lakes on the eastern shore of Lake Erie are grown the French hybrid grapes with names like Seyve-Villard, Seibel 5299 or Baco #1.

Meanwhile, in California, there are such French varieties as Pinot Chardonnay, Cabernet Sauvignon, Ravat Blanc, Seyval, Johannisburg Riesling and Pinot Noir.

Among the newcomers, one of the fastest growing grape areas in the United States are the states of Washington and Oregon. Both hold great possibilities for the true lover of viniculture.

While it is possible to purchase quality concentrates or juices in cans or purchase whole fruit, you cannot win your "Purple Thumb" until you have pressed your own fruit. There is something uniquely satisfying in making the red fluid burst forth from the grape with press handle in hand, or if you really want the greatest pleasure of all, invite a neighborly Sophia to some barefoot tromping in a tub.

The proper selection of grapes is of paramount importance in making red wine or, for that matter, any wine. The world's greatest grapes for red wine are Pinot Noir and Cabernet Sauvignon. Unfortunately, these grapes have been grown domestically with much success only in California's Napa Valley. Success is probably a very appropriate word. Within the past 50 years, California has enjoyed an unprecedented housing boom, resulting in vast acreages that were once vineyards being converted by land developers into huge housing tracts. In general, the builders were able to pay the vineyard owner more money for his land than he was able to make in harvesting grapes. However, with the ever-growing popularity of wine, some vineyards are beginning to be worth far more money as vineyards than as housing tracts. Some of the best producing vineyards are selling for as much as $20,000 an acre! So, if you decide to embark on an interesting and worthwhile hobby, grape growing might be an answer.

The French hybrid grapes also make excellent red wines. These hybrids evolved in the early 1900's from the efforts of French grape growers to combine the sturdy American grape, which had excellent disease and insect resistance, with the high-quality European grape. The Frenchmen who crossed (or hybridized) these grape strains had names like: Baco, Seibel, Millet, Seyve-Villard. Consequently, their names became associated with certain strains of grapes. These grapes have now been grown in this country for a quarter of a century and are among the choicest in the world for making wine. Grapes from these vines are high in natural sugar, have a nearly ideal acid content and, more importantly, possess outstanding flavor.

The American grape strains, while being slightly less noble, tend to have higher crop yields and are more adapted to withstand the severe North American climate and soil conditions. And, do not sell these American grapes short, because many of the finest champagnes in the world are produced from some of them.

The following are some of the types of grapes that will also make excellent red wine:

In the northeastern states, the most common grape variety is the Concord. This grape grows well in even the severest climate and is generally plentiful in crop yield. However, it is not considered a good wine grape due to its high acidic content and "foxy" flavor. In spite of these apparent drawbacks, many people are still quite fond of it. When using Concord grapes, it is a good idea to dilute the juice (one part of water to two parts of juice) before fermentation. Better bets for red wine include the French Hybrids—Chelois, Baco Noir, Seibel #7053, etc., which, unfortunately, are more expensive and more difficult to grow.

As we have mentioned, the best grapes in the western states for making red wine are: Cabernet Sauvignon and Pinot Noir. Other excellent varieties include Zinfandel, Gamay, Grenache, Ruby Cabernet, Rubired, Royalty, and Salvador.

Grape growing has never been carried on extensively in the southern United States, but the Muscadine and Scuppernong grapes can provide good wines.

4. An Aside to the Newcomer—It is our goal to help you make home wines that will rival and even surpass commercial wines. This, we are frank to admit, is a tall order, but a number of home winemakers have already achieved just such a goal, and with some patience, diligence and a little luck, you can as well.

One of the basic problems the home winemaking newcomer faces is the number of available alternatives for making wine that make the whole process appear to be quite complex. Actually, this is as it should be since this is one of the major reasons why winemaking has become so popular. A wine hobbyist can choose his own method based on his interest, needs and resources. He can "do his own thing" as is oft said. However, we feel it is our job to simplify the winemaking process for the newcomer as much as possible. We hope to remove some of the mystique that surrounds winemaking. We do use the word "some" because another reason why winemaking is so popular is that it is so steeped in mystique. It is our aim to make what is basically a complex process as simple as possible for the newcomer, who will find as he gains experience and increases his winemaking skills that there are always new challenges to face.

The winemaking hobby is much like wine since it continually is changing. It never stays the same. Here, there is no such thing as status quo.

To help you meet the goal of making superior wines, we have organized our book along the lines of the basic steps in winemaking from "Selecting the Fruit" to "Serving the Wine."

We have supplied complete and accurate descriptions of all the various pieces of equipment and processes that can be used in winemaking and have included guidelines for their use. Many of these descriptions are illustrations and, since they are in sequential order, we suggest you begin your reading by flipping through these illustrations—starting from the front and working your way through to the back. In this way, you will gain an overall picture of the entire winemaking process in a very short period of time.

Since every specialized activity, such as golf, bridge and stamp collecting, winemaking being no exception, has a language all its own, we also suggest you start your reading by scanning the glossary that is located in the back of this book. To become a thoroughly knowledgeable winemaker, you must be familiar with winemaking terminology.

And, finally, we suggest you read both the red and white wine chapters completely and thoroughly before attempting to make any wine. The two processes are basically the same, but there are some very important differences which you should be aware of.

Part Two:

Red Wine

Red table wine is one of the better wines for the newcomer to home winemaking to get started with as he will rarely fail to make a passable one. Naturally, as in making all wines, there are varying degrees of success, but the majority of homemade red dinner wines are at least palatable.

Red dinner wines are more astringent and full-bodied than most other wines since the whole grape is used during primary fermentation. In contrast, only the juice is used when making white wines.

One question that frequently pops up is, "How does red wine get its color?" The red in red wines does not have as much relationship to the color of the grape as is generally believed. Red wines can be made from red, purple or black grapes. The red in red wine is imparted by processing rather than the color of the grape. There are two possible processes that can extract the red color. The grapes may be heated before processing, or the grape skins may be included in the fermentation process.

5. Crushing the Grapes—In preparing the fruit, a mixture of pectic enzyme and water should be sprinkled over the grapes at least three hours before crushing. Pectic enzymes work on the pectin contained in all fruit juices. Pectin is the material that holds the fruit fibers together. By breaking the pectin down, the fruit becomes easier to press. This treatment will also provide a higher juice yield and improve the color and clarity of the wine. Pectic enzyme is available in tablet or powdered form which, when used, is mixed with water. For each bushel of fruit to be pressed, mix seven 8-grain tablets or one teaspoon of powder in about 3 ounces of water.

As previously mentioned, the red color in red wine is obtained by processing rather than the color of the grapes. The red color may be produced either by heating the grapes or by using the skins during fermentation.

Numerous commercial wineries initially crush the grapes, putting both the juice and skins through a heat exchanger and cooking at 140°. Then, the skins and juice are quickly placed into a press with the juice being separated from the skins by the pressing action. Such pressed juice has a reddish brown tinge which eventually results in red wine.

The home winemaker can obtain approximately the same results by heating the grapes before crushing them. This preliminary heating will help to develop the dark red color of the wine. Grapes may be heated by either of two methods. The most practical way is to place a basket of grapes in your kitchen oven and warm them at 140°-160°F for about 30 minutes. Then remove them and press immediately.

We have found that a great deal of the fun, mystery, and continual search for better ways to make wine can be attributed to this particular operation. As we have already mentioned, winemaking is both an art and a science. It can safely be said that no one person has all the answers. You can get as much expert opinion on how to make wine as there are experts making their own. Some knowledgeable home winemakers state categorically that you should never heat grapes since heating will reduce the subsequent wine's flavor and aroma. Other experts state, however, that you should heat the grapes for precisely 15 seconds and then remove and press them. Others just as strongly feel that you should cook them for at least six hours!

Red Wine

Another method of heating grapes is to dip them in hot water for ten minutes and then remove and press. Many home winemakers prefer this approach because they feel the grapes aren't cooked, and, therefore, don't lose their flavor.

Your own success in making fine wines will depend upon your combining the right mix of art and science. You will find success also depends to a great extent on trial and error.

We personally prefer to include the wine skins in the fermentation for several reasons. First, it is generally quite difficult to control heating the grapes and, if you are not particularly careful and exercise tight controls, the grapes may become overcooked with the resultant wine having a caramel flavor. More importantly, including wine skins during fermentation results in a natural dark red wine. Actually, it is entirely possible to develop a homemade wine that is darker and redder in color than wines made by commercial wineries. Since appearance is especially important in winemaking, utilizing the skins is almost a necessity.

Another area of controversy arises in the preparation of the grape. Some very experienced winemaking hobbyists feel the grapes should be washed to remove all traces of dirt, wild yeast and insecticides. Their recommended course of action is to simply wash the fruit in cool water as if it were to be eaten. On the other hand, some home-winemaking experts feel the grapes should be left unwashed. They believe washing destroys some of the grapes inherent ingredients, such as natural yeast that appears on the skins and which should be included in making a good wine.

We are inclined to go along with the first suggestion, that is, wash the grapes in cool water to remove dirt and insecticides—but don't scrub them!

17

There is general agreement that the grape stems should be removed when making red wine, particularly if you plan to use the grape skins in primary fermentation, since the stems may add a very bitter taste to the wine. In addition, all spoiled, or about to be spoiled, grapes should be removed.

After removing the stems, place the unwashed grapes in a bag, aptly called "a pressing bag." Put this bag in a grape press similar to the one *illustrated on page 21*. The juice is then pressed from the grapes into a "primary fermenter container." After several pressings, the bag is removed from the grape press and the grape skins are taken from the bag and added to the juice already in the container. The grape press is by far the easiest, most professional, and convenient method of preparing the juice.

It is also possible to use a Helical Grinder or a Squeezo Press similar to those *illustrated on page 23*. Here, the grapes are first fed into a hopper and then crushed into a "primary fermenter."

Instead of using the above, it is also possible to use a fruit crusher such as those *illustrated on page 25*. The grapes are fed into the crusher's hopper and then crushed between its rollers. These rollers are rotated by a hand crank, giving you the opportunity to demonstrate your manual dexterity. After passing through the rollers, grape juice and skins alike drop into a container (the primary fermenter container) which is located directly beneath the apparatus. Any remaining grapes that aren't crushed by their passing through the rollers of the fruit crusher can be picked out and crushed by hand. However, be sure to wear rubber gloves when crushing by hand to avoid staining your hands with the acids present in some fruits.

As a last possibility, if you don't have either a Helical Grinder, Squeezo Press, or a fruit crusher, don't despair; you can always use your hands, feet, a potato masher, or even a wooden two-by-four that has been left over from your last building job. A very effective method of crushing small quantities of grapes is to place them in a plastic bucket and flail away with a two-by-four.

GRAPE PRESSES

For those of you who plan to go into winemaking in a relatively big way, a grape press is almost a necessity. The basket-styled presses that are shown on the opposite page are sturdily constructed of selected hardwood—red oak. The larger press can handle up to 200 lbs. of grapes at one time. This press is the answer to those of you who own your own vineyard or who want to share a press with your neighbors.

The smaller press will handle a bushel of grapes per hour and should prove ideal for those of you who plan to only press a few bushels.

TYPICAL PRESSES

Press Type	P1	P2	P3	P4	P5
Diameter of Basket	9″	10″	12″	16″	18″
Height of Basket	11″	15″	18″	22″	24″
Overall Height	21″	38″	43″	53″	56″
Shipping Weight	30#	60#	90#	145#	235#
Capacity—Crushed	60#	150#	250#	500#	800#

Red Wine

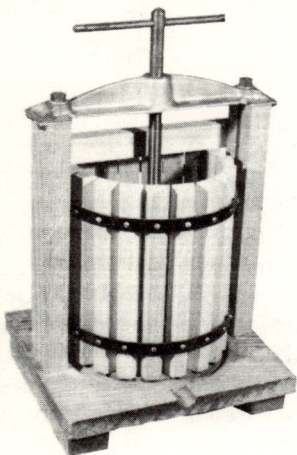

HELICAL GRINDER

The Helical Grinder is a compact unit that operates on the same helical cone principle used in the crushers in commercial wineries, and will extract 99% of the juice from your grapes. The grinder is crank operated and attaches to a smooth surface with vacuum-cup feet. In addition to grapes, cherries, etc., it can be used to squeeze the juices from vegetables, and comes with meat grinding attachments which extend its versatility.

SQUEEZO PRESS

The Squeezo Press is similar to the Helical Grinder in the way it operates, has a larger capacity including an extra-large hopper for the fruit to be crushed. It is easy to operate, and has a self-lubricating brass bushing along with double bearings for easy crushing. The unit is fast and uses a wooden plunger to feed the material into the crusher. Juice flows out the strainer spout, while seeds, stems, and dry pulp are carried out through the front. The unit clamps to the edge of a table. In addition to its use in winemaking, it can also double as a handy device for making applesauce and other purees that will delight the family at dinnertime.

HELICAL GRINDER

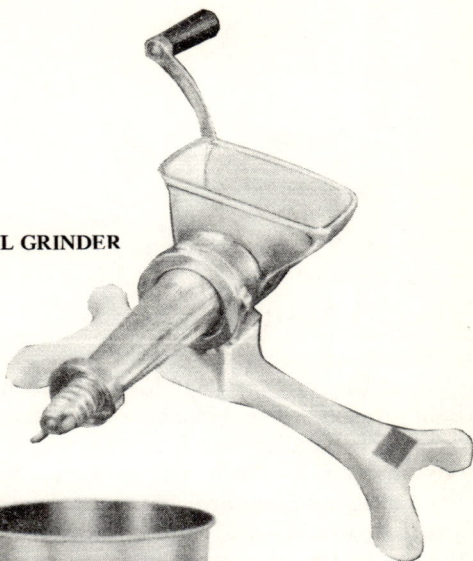

SQUEEZO PRESS

FRUIT CRUSHERS

If you wish to crush apples, pears, peaches, etc., as well as grapes, you should consider using a quality-built crusher. The crushers illustrated have red oak hardwood handles and frames (except for the crusher on the bottom, which has an aluminum hopper). All units have aluminum rollers and are mounted on frames so that you can place them on top of a barrel to catch the crushed grapes. We highly recommend this type of unit if you will be using a large quantity of firm fruit as well as grapes. These units will give excellent service and all are easy to use.

FRUIT CRUSHERS

STEAM JUICER

A typical Steam Juicer is shown on the next page. With this type of unit you can extract the juice rather effortlessly. In addition, the juice is already pasteurized and can be used for winemaking with less concern about exposure to wild yeasts. This unit is extremely well-suited for dealing with dried fruits, which are today becoming more popular with winemakers because you can make dried fruit wine throughout the year. This particular unit is made from pure aluminum and is easy to use and clean. It will last for a long time. Such a unit is ideally suited for making many other kinds of juices, also.

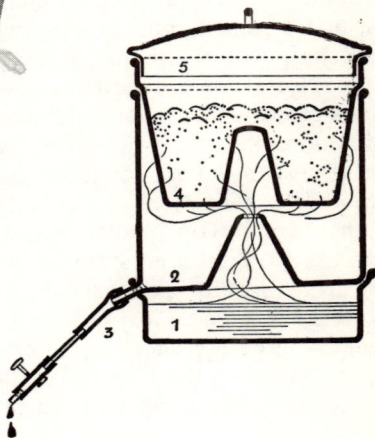

STEAM JUICER

27

6. Treating the Juice—Here is the step in the winemaking process where care and patient thoughtfulness really pay off! We are at the fork in the road where one path leads to a superhighway that will whisk us off to "Vin Ordinaire," while the other slow, thorough route will take us to "Vin Premier Grand Classe." If your only object is to make some wine, it is all quite simple—toss in some yeast and sugar, put on the fermentation lock, and Mother Nature will bail you out by producing something passable. Occasionally, such haphazardness will even turn out quite well. But, for the consistent production of fine wine, study and thorough preparation are a must! This route is not the one that everyone cares to follow, however, but for those who will take the extra time to pursue it, they will be more than amply rewarded.

All fruit juices contain water, sugar, tartaric, citric, or malic acid, essential or aromatic oils, certain minerals, and starch. Grapes containing these ingredients in ideal proportions are the great grapes of the world: Pinot Noir, Pinot Chardonnay, Riesling, and a few others grown under ideal conditions of climate, weather, soil, and cultivation. These are the grapes that provide the utmost in flavor, bouquet, body, aftertaste, and all the other qualities that expert tasters seek and demand of their wine. Top quality grapes need no help from man except a cultured strain of yeast. All other grapes and fruits require assistance from the chemist, be he professional or not, to produce a good wine. The two steps required are checking and adjusting the acid and sugar content of the juice. Also, before fermentation is started, it is important to sterilize the juice.

Red Wine

Checking Acid Content—It is important to think about *acid* content. All fruits are somewhat acidic—some more than others. When tasting the juice, acidity is not always noticeable, since it is often masked by the juice's sweetness. However, when most of the sugar has been fermented to alcohol, the acid content becomes starkly apparent. For example, wine made from orange juice is exceedingly bitter unless steps have been taken to offset or dilute the acid. However, all wines should have some acid (the ideal being between .5 and .75% by volume). Its content, together with any residual sugar, will determine the wine's ultimate sweetness or dryness.

Excessive acidity may be corrected by dilution (but unfortunately this procedure also dilutes the sugar, color, and essential oils), or by adding calcium carbonate. Deficient acidity is corrected by adding tartaric, malic, or citric acid. To precisely determine the acid content of the juice and the amount of correction needed, titration equipment is essential. However, it is possible to use graduated indicator papers, that will provide you with an approximate range.

Available professional equipment is *illustrated on pages 61 and 62*. You can also make your own. If you decide to do it yourself, the necessary parts may be purchased from many wine supply dealers.

To make your own testing apparatus, you will need a 50 ml buret with a scale graduated in tenths, and a 10 ml pipette. You will also need a stand to hold the buret plus a few clamps to secure it and a glass or stainless steel stirring rod. You will also require a 1/10th normal solution of sodium hydroxide (chemical formula, NaOH) and another chemical called phenolphthalein which can be poured into a dropper bottle. Finally, you will need a bottle of distilled water or boiled tap water.

After filling your buret with sodium hydroxide (NaOH), open its stopcock and allow some NaOH to run out to remove trapped air. Note the amount of NaOH remaining in the buret by reading the bottom of the curve formed by the liquid in the glass and mark it down accordingly. Allow about 10 ml of NaOH per test of juice sample. Now, use the pipette to place 10 ml of the juice to be tested into a beaker. Next, add a few drops of phenolphthalein and stir the mixture.

The next step is to slowly open the stopcock on the buret and allow the NaOH to drip, drop by drop, into the beaker's solution, stirring or swirling the water solution constantly. Continue to stir the solution until it develops a light pink color. When it does, stop! If the pink coloration immediately disappears, add another drop or two of NaOH and determine if the color remains for 20 to 30 seconds. If it does, then go onto the next step—reading the amount of NaOH in the buret. Record this amount and subtract it from the initial reading to determine the amount of NaOH that has been used. Finally, multiply the quantity that has been used by .075 to calculate the % acid. For example, suppose your buret read 45 ml at the start of your test and 38 ml NaOH at the end. This means you used 7 ml NaOH during the test. Therefore, you have the following mathematical solution:

$$(45 \text{ ml} - 38 \text{ ml}) \times .075 = .525\%$$

An ideal acid content is .7%. If the juice is too acid, add calcium carbonate and/or water. If too low, add acid. Each 1½ teaspoons of calcium carbonate will lower the acid content of a gallon of wine by about .1%. Do not add more than three teaspoons per gallon or the taste of the wine will be adversely affected. Beyond this point, dilute with water.

If it is necessary to add acid, 1 teaspoon of tartaric acid will raise the acid content of a gallon of wine by about .1%. For the best taste, a blend of tartaric, citric, and malic acids is generally preferred.

Checking Sugar Content—Normally, natural wines do not exceed 14% alcohol because most yeasts die at that concentration of alcohol. Yeast, of course, is the substance that converts the juice sugar into alcohol and carbon dioxide. Juice that has a 24% sugar content will make wine having a 14% alcohol concentration, while juice having 20% sugar will produce wine with an 11% alcohol content. Juice with a sugar concentration of less than 20% will become a wine that is low in alcohol content and therefore subject to spoilage. Juice with a sugar content of more than 25% will be overly sweet since all of the sugar will not ferment. The ideal sugar content for red wine is considered by most authorities to be about 24%.

Therefore, you have to determine the sugar content of the "must" that is ready for fermentation. Obviously, sugar content is of immense importance since it determines the wine's alcohol content. A high alcohol content is desirable, not just because we are trying to make an alcoholic beverage, but because alcohol is needed to preserve and stabilize the wine. The best method of determining sugar content is to use a professional instrument called a hydrometer which is *illustrated on page 57*. This instrument will let you know when the sugar content is ideal. It will help you decide how much sugar to add to raise the sugar content or the amount of water dilution needed to bring it down.

Basically, a hydrometer is that familiar instrument that your favorite service station attendant uses to measure the amount of anti-freeze in your car's radiator. His hydrometer has a closed glass tube with a weighted ball on one end and a rolled paper scale inside. A wine hydrometer, on the other hand, has a measuring scale called a Brix scale. To help you to better understand this device, let's assume you want to test a bottle of distilled water for sugar content. First, lower the hydrometer into the distilled water. The Brix scale reading should be 0, since distilled water doesn't contain any sugar. For comparison's sake, let's assume that your grape juice and skins have a sugar content of 18%. After drawing off a sample of the juice, you then lower your hydrometer into the juice and receive a reading of 18% on the Brix scale. (The hydrometer rises to where the scale reads 18%.) Basically, the higher the solution's sugar content, the higher the hydrometer will float.

Some wine hydrometers have a specific gravity scale. If this type of wine hydrometer were lowered into distilled water, which is basically pure, containing no minerals, the reading on the specific gravity scale would be 1.000. If you were to use this same hydrometer to test your grape juice that had 18% sugar, the specific gravity scale would read 1.082. In some cases the term gravity is used in place of specific gravity. Gravity is simply a cryptic shortening of the two words. A gravity reading of 82 is the same as a specific gravity reading of 1.082.

One of the most practical hydrometers available is the one that is *shown on page 57*. It has three scales on its stem: a Brix scale, a specific gravity scale, and a potential percentage of alcohol scale. Needless to say, it's quite complete and simple to use.

Red Wine

In testing for sugar content, a testing jar should be used in conjunction with the hydrometer. (*Illustrated on page 57.*) Fill the testing jar two-thirds full with grape juice. Then, obtain your reading on the hydrometer by lowering the weighted end into the grape juice in the testing jar.

As we have noted, 24% is the ideal Brix scale reading for making red wine. To determine the amount of sugar that you must add to your grape juice, find the Brix scale reading of your juice and record the amount. Then, calculate the amount of sugar that must be added by subtracting your juice's Brix scale % from 24. *For each full percentage point difference, add 2 ounces (¼ cup) of sugar per gallon of juice.*

This calculation can be expressed as a convenient formula:

$$\text{cups of sugar to be added} = \text{gallons of juice} \times \left\{ \frac{24 - \text{measured Brix}}{4} \right\}$$

The ultimate in sugar testing equipment is the saccharimeter, *pictured on page 57.* The saccharimeter, which works on the difference in light refraction of different sugar concentrations, has an added advantage in that it not only can be used to test grape juice, but it can also be used to test the sugar content of grapes while they are still on the vine.

In summation, adding water to the juice reduces sugar content and adding sugar raises it. To measure sugar concentration, use either a hydrometer or a saccharimeter. Don't try to test by just tasting the juice! A low-acid juice with only 12% sugar may taste sweeter than a high-acid juice with a 22% content. Resist sampling the juice until a later time.

7. Sterilizing the Juice—Grapes are generally covered with wild yeasts which are whitish in color and are called "bloom." Since these yeasts do not aid in the fermentation process, they should be killed by the addition of sulfur dioxide. Sulfur dioxide comes from either potassium metabisulfite or sodium bisulfite. Both are available from wine supply houses. When using either of these chemicals, we recommend making a stock solution and keeping it on hand so that it is available when needed. To make a sulfur dioxide solution, dissolve five tablespoons of potassium metabisulfite in one quart of water. Keep the container that holds this water and metabisulfite closed (or stoppered) and full. We suggest you make a fresh solution every three months and throw out any old ones still on hand. When mixed with your juice, ¾ of a teaspoon added to 1 gallon of juice will contribute about 50 parts per million (ppm) of sulfur dioxide (SO_2).

Instead of making a bisulfite solution, it is possible to use bisulfite (Campden) tablets. All that you need to do is add one Campden tablet per wine gallon. Since these tablets are readily available from wine supply dealers, it is by far the easiest and most convenient method. If the fruit that you purchased to make the juice was particularly overripe, add two Campden tablets per gallon instead of one. Each tablet adds 50 parts per million of SO_2 to the juice, which is enough to kill wild yeast but not the cultured yeast. It is a good idea to crush these tablets in a separate container and then dissolve by adding water and stirring thoroughly. Then add the dissolved tablets to the juice. For best results, add the tablets at least four hours before you add the yeast.

8. Fermenting—*An Overview*—The central and most important single aspect of winemaking is fermentation. It is the process by which yeast go about their mysterious work of converting a sugar-containing juice into wine. Even in our era of advanced technology, wine is not made by man. It is made by nature, itself, working in submicroscopic obscurity. However, the results are clearly visible—and quite dramatic—to those who have observed the process through a transparent fermentation tank. Man prepares the juice, adds the yeast, and provides the proper environment. The yeast cells do the rest.

Starting with a small culture added to the prepared juice, the yeast multiply through many generations while consuming the sugar and converting it to alcohol and carbon dioxide gas. At first, when the sugar concentration is high, the yeast multiply rapidly, and the fermentation action is vigorous. As the sugar is used up, the succeeding generations of yeast become smaller and the fermentation activity declines. When the sugar is entirely consumed or the alcohol content reaches the concentration in which yeast cannot live, fermentation is complete.

Technically, when fermentation stops, the product is wine. However, only the impatient novice would try to bottle or drink it at that time. As experience is gained, the winemaker will set himself higher standards and strive for better wine, and hence will allow adequate aging. Chemists identify the end-product of fermentation as a mixture of literally hundreds of different kinds of alcohols, aldehydes, and esters. Furthermore, they know that the slow interaction of these chemicals in the presence of slight amounts of oxygen produce new chemicals which wine experts agree improve the taste and flavor. This is about as much as is known. The aging process of wine has engaged the best minds of the world for centuries, but even now there is only a limited understanding. Suffice it to say, aging is important, and the successful winemaker will not rush the process.

While slight amounts of oxygen are important in aging, air is the winemaker's greatest enemy, and the importance of protecting wine from the air cannot be exaggerated. The mycoderma aceti and the vinegar fly that carries it must be avoided at all cost. The water-seal valve or fermentation lock is the surest protection. During the early, vigorous stages of fermentation, some winemakers prefer an open crock for ease of handling and avoidance of overflowing. This method, if used correctly, also will stimulate a very active yeast growth. However, it is probably less risky to conduct fermentation in a vessel guarded at all times with a fermentation lock. Such a water seal can be left in place right on through the aging process.

There are three general types of fermentation vessels other than crocks. They are: wooden barrels, glass jugs or carboys, and polyethylene tanks. Wooden barrels seem to have the ideal degree of oxygen permeability for aging, but they are relatively expensive and require a fair amount of maintenance. Glass jugs are rather easy to keep clean, but they present breakage problems, and, of course, are not porous enough to permit small amounts of oxygen to aid in the aging process. Polyethylene tanks are preferred by a growing number of winemakers because they have about the same oxygen permeability as wooden barrels, are lightweight, are relatively easy to clean, and are less expensive.

Adding Yeast—Enzyme or *yeast* chemistry takes us to the frontier of man's knowledge. Yeast cells are microscopic organisms that fill both the air and soil around us. Their varieties are countless, and they behave in many different ways. One of their common characteristics is that they can consume one or more chemicals and convert them into one or more different chemicals. The yeast types of interest to the winemaker are those that will convert sugar (and, to a lesser degree, the other ingredients of fruit juice) into alcohol and carbon dioxide gas (and to some extent, desirable essential oils).

We do not recommend Baker's yeast or bread yeast even though it will do a passable job of making wine. This type of yeast results in a violent fermentation that will tend to reduce the final aroma of the wine. Wine made from these yeasts will even have a faint odor or taste of fresh bread. Moreover, bread yeast is very intolerant to alcohol or sulfur dioxide or, for that matter, sugar, and will produce a light, fluffy sediment in your final product that is both undesirable and highly unattractive.

Purchasing a special wine yeast (cultured yeast) is a wise investment since it will provide good flavor and will help to ensure complete fermentation. The different types of yeast are distinguished by the essential oils they produce or leave behind. Each type is the result of decades or even centuries of experimentation to find those yeast strains that will do their job best. For a long time, these yeasts were the private, secret property of various individual wineries. Today, not only are these yeasts available to everyone, but recently they have become available in a dry form with a long shelf life, thereby enabling home winemakers everywhere to share more easily the secrets of the master vintners of the old world.

Yeast is the agent that kicks off the fermentation. To start this process, add a small culture of yeast to the grape juice. The yeast cells then multiply by feeding on the sugar and nutrients of the juice. At first, when the sugar content is high, the yeast cells will multiply rapidly. This activity will slow down as the sugar is consumed and, when it is used up or the alcohol reaches a concentration lethal to the yeast (14%), fermentation is completed, resulting in the product, wine.

There are three ways that yeast is available: in dry form, in liquid form and agar slants. Dry yeast is usually packaged in 5-gram foil containers. A 5-gram foil packet is enough yeast to start fermentation of 5 gallons of grape juice. However, to insure rapid fermentation, the yeast should first be added to a small amount of water or juice in a separate kitchen pan that has been warmed. The yeast should be allowed about 10 minutes to activate, and then this mixture should be poured into the container holding the juice.

It is also possible to stretch the 5 grams of yeast over a greater amount of juice. If, for example, you are making 50 gallons of wine, you can prepare a mixture called a yeast starter or culture and proportion this mixture out among the containers holding the grape juice to make 50 gallons of wine.

One of the biggest advantages of dry yeast is that it will keep for long periods of time. If kept in a refrigerator, it can be preserved for as long as one year.

The second type of yeast is in a liquid form and is sealed in a small glass vial. These yeasts are designed to produce a specific type of wine such as Chablis, Burgundy, and Rhine wine, and are added to a yeast starter solution.

The third and last type of yeast is called agar slants. They are supplied in a test tube which is seeded with specific yeast strains. The shelf life of yeast on an agar slant is short—probably not longer than three to four months.

To prepare a yeast starter, draw off some of the grape juice into a separate container. Then, add some bisulfite and approximately four hours later add three table-spoons of a sugar-water solution. On top of this, add three more cups of water. Boil this mixture slowly for about five minutes. The boiling will kill any wild juices present. Then, pour the mixture into a scalding hot jug or bottle and allow it to cool to 100°F. Check the temperature with a thermometer. Add the special wine yeast and just a pinch of yeast nutrient. Now, shake the jug vigorously and stopper the top with a clean rag. (This stopper can act as the regular water lock.) Then, put this jug in a warm place and maintain the temperature between 70°-80°F for two or three days. At the end of this time, the mixture should have started to foam due to CO_2 released by the yeast's breaking down of the sugars. The yeast starter is now ready to be poured into each five gallons of your juice for the start of fermentation.

Adding Yeast Nutrient—The sugar in fruit juice is the principal "food" for yeast cells. However, a diet of sugar alone, while enough to sustain life (as in intravenous feeding in humans), does not provide robust health for yeast. Therefore, it is important to add yeast *nutrient* in all cases where sugar has been added. Yeast nutrient contains nitrogen, phosphorous, and Vitamin B1, and its use will maximize alcohol content by preventing premature cessation of fermentation (often referred to as a "stuck" fermentation).

Fermentation—Reviewing where we are for a moment, the crushed grapes are lying in a container and have already been treated for acid and sugar, sterilized, and yeast is ready to be added to start the fermentation process. It is possible to complete fermentation by either one of two methods. Some winemakers prefer to conduct their fermentation in two stages, "primary" and "secondary." The primary fermentation is normally conducted in an open crock and is the very active stage. Secondary fermentation is a slower, quieter stage that must be conducted in a container sealed with a fermentation lock.

With a few precautions, the two stages are not really necessary and fermentation can be completed by using just one type of container such as the very popular polyethylene tanks called cubitainers (*illustrated on page 47*).

Winemaking can be made remarkably easy by using these cubitainers which are available from most distributors and dealers of winemaking supplies. They are compact and can be used conveniently in apartments where space is at a premium and equally as well in houses where space is not a particular problem. It is also possible to complete the fermentation process in one step by using the polyethylene jugs that are *illustrated on page 49*.

If you do decide to use either of these containers, it will be necessary to use a funnel during the crushing operation so that both the juice and skins flow smoothly into the top opening. Then prepare the yeast according to the instructions on the packet and add to the juice. *See discussion, page 66.* It is particularly important that all containers be thoroughly cleaned with soap and warm water and finally rinsed with cold clean water before filling. In filling the cubitainer (or whatever) with juice and skins, be sure to leave about an inch of space at the top to allow room for foaming during fermentation.

The fermentation process is now ready to start. However, it is important to protect the juice from the air, since both oxygen and airborne contaminants can cause spoilage. A water-seal valve (or fermentation lock) is ideal for this purpose since it is designed to release the mounting carbon-dioxide gas pressure produced during fermentation without letting any air reach the juice.

To set up your fermentation lock, fill the valve with water to its mid-point. Then, screw it into place over the mouth of the tank. This arrangement lets gas escape, but does not allow outside air to reach the juice. (*See illustration on page 65.*)

Fermentation usually begins within 24 hours after the yeast is added and will become evident with the appearance of gas bubbling in the water-seal valve. (In a warm room, it will start sooner than in a cool room. The ideal temperature is 60°-70°F.) If fermentation does not start within 3 days, check to be sure the valve is screwed tightly to the tank. Also, during the first few days, check the water-seal tube several times to be sure that it is not blocked by either foam or fruit skins. Check, too, to see that the tank is not overflowing.

If overflowing does occur, remove the foam by squeezing the tank. If possible, move it to a cooler place. Should overflowing persist, divide the juice among additional tanks or pour it into a clean plastic bucket and cover with a sheet of plastic. After heavy foaming subsides in a day or two, pour it back into the tank and cap with a water-seal.

It is also possible to use the traditional wooden barrel such as those *illustrated on page 51*. However, barrels are not too practical in view of the improved, modern equipment available today. Wooden wine barrels are usually not airtight so that the winemaker must continually worry about air leaks ruining his wine. In addition, wooden wine barrels are opaque, so the winemaker cannot see how his wine is doing. Proper maintenance of wine barrels is of paramount importance and is one of the biggest drawbacks to their use. Maintenance is *discussed on page 52*.

Fermentation is normally quite active initially, but, within a week, it should have passed its peak and start to diminish, ceasing altogether in 3 to 6 weeks. Fermentation is essentially complete at this time and clarification can be started.

If you wish to avoid the risk of overflow, you may decide to go through the steps of primary and then secondary fermentation. One possible container that can be used as a primary fermenter is the polyethylene crock that is *illustrated on page 49*. If you decide to use this crock, only fill it about three-quarters full since some overflowing may occur during the violent primary fermentation. As an extra precaution, place the crock on a pan.

If you do not have an open crock, it is possible to use a plastic garbage can, a plastic laundry pail, or a wooden barrel that has been cut in half. Simply transfer the pressed juice (plus the skins, if you are making red wine) to the vessel being used as a primary fermenter.

Cover the primary fermenter with a cloth or a thin sheet of polyethylene (plastic) material. A plastic garbage disposal bag makes an ideal cover. Then, put the fermenter in a location where the temperature does not drop below 60° nor exceed 74°-76°F. In about 10 hours' time, you will notice fermentation beginning as small particles of foam begin to collect. In another two days, a full, rolling fermentation should start with quite active foaming. You should allow this fermentation to continue until the foaming subsides. It will take between four to seven days for this to occur. At this time, the contents should be transferred to the secondary fermenter. In addition, remove the grape stems and skins at this time. As we have mentioned, skins are left in the juice while making red wine, because they add red color to the wine. However, if the skins are left with the juice for too long a period, they contribute excessive tannin to the juice resulting in a bitter tasting wine. Furthermore, during fermentation, the grape skins and pulp may rise to the top and form what is known as a "cap." This cap should be punched down at least once a day. In commercial wineries, this cap can become so thick that it becomes quite difficult to punch down.

To remove the skins from the juice, you must use a press. Both the wine juice and skins are ladled or bailed from the primary fermenter and placed in the press. The juice is then squeezed into another container. When pressing, apply pressure slowly and allow the juice to run out through a siphon into the second container. After pressing once, release the pressure, stir the remaining pulp in the press, and repeat the process. Continue to stir and press until you have all the juice squeezed out of the pulp. (Pulp is also called pomace.) Timing is important during pressing since the less time the juice is exposed to air, the less opportunity there is for it to turn to vinegar.

Secondary fermentation will proceed much more slowly for several weeks or even months. During this interval, it is important to protect the wine from air to prevent spoilage. Therefore, the secondary fermenter should be a vessel with a small opening into which a fermentation lock (described earlier) can be placed. For this purpose, glass carboys, wooden barrels, or cubitainers or other polyethylene tanks can be used.

The wine should be left in the secondary fermenter until the sugar has been completely changed to alcohol and the wine has had a chance to age somewhat. If the sugar content was 24% to begin with, the sugar is completely converted when the specific gravity of the wine gets down to .9903. At this point, the wine is ready for clarification and bottling. If the measurements are unknown or cannot be made, a simple rule of thumb is to allow at least 3 months for secondary fermentation.

Summation—The sequential steps in treating the juice are: (1) check and adjust acid content of juice, (2) check and adjust sugar content of juice, (3) add sodium or potassium metabisulfite, (4) prepare and add yeast, (5) add yeast nutrient, and (6) allow juice to ferment.

FERMENTATION VESSELS

CUBITAINERS

Cubitainers made with strong, durable polyethylene plastic are rapidly becoming the most popular vessels for fermenting and aging. They have many singular advantages in that they are lightweight and easy to store; are translucent, permitting easy viewing of the fermentation process; are easy to clean and resistant to breakage; and are low priced. They are equipped with a standard 38mm screw opening and cap, and are available in several sizes: 1 gallon, 2½ gallon, 5 gallon.

Up to 25 bottles of wine at a time can be made in the 5-gallon cubitainer. The 2½-gallon container makes 12 bottles of wine, while the 1-gallon container makes 5 bottles. The containers shown have water-seal valves attached which allow fermentation without danger of exposure to air.

POLYETHYLENE CUBITAINERS

**CUBITAINERS FILLED WITH
WINE JUICE**

RIGID POLYETHYLENE JUGS

The rigid polyethylene jugs have some of the same advantages as the cubitainers except that they cannot be collapsed for storage and are not as easy to clean. However, they are easier to transport when filled since they are rigid and come equipped with a handle.

5-GAL. RIGID POLYETHYLENE JUG—
Wide-Mouth Opening

The 5-gallon rigid polyethylene heavy duty jug is equipped with a 63mm opening, which is a very helpful feature when loading whole grapes or other fruits into the tank. In addition, the jug has a molded handle for ease in transporting.

PRIMARY FERMENTATION VESSELS (*Crocks*)

Some winemakers prefer to conduct the first few days' fermentation, when activity is at a peak, in an open crock to foster rapid yeast growth and to avoid overflowing.

Red Wine

**RIGID POLYETHYLENE –
38MM OPENING**

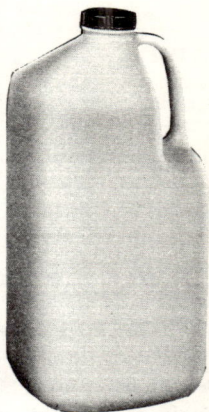

**5-GAL. RIGID POLYETHYLENE JUG –
WIDE-MOUTH OPENING**

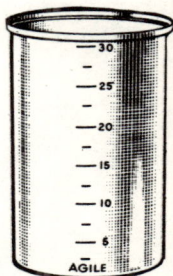

**PRIMARY FERMENTATION VESSELS
(CROCKS)**

49

BARRELS

The classic fermentation and aging vessel that has been used throughout the world for centuries is, of course, the oak barrel. It is strong, will last for generations, has ideal oxygen permeability properties, and is available in large sizes. On the other hand, barrels are heavy, more costly, and require regular maintenance to prevent leakage and bacterial contamination. Barrels come either waxed or charred. Waxed barrels are less likely to leak as they become older, but charred barrels are thought to impart better aging. The barrels are generally available in the following sizes: 1 gallon, 2 gallon, 5 gallon, 10 gallon, 15 gallon, 20 gallon and 30 gallon.

SPIGOTS

A tap or faucet on the aging tank is useful in that it permits the wine to be drawn off without disturbing the sediment. There are two types: polyethylene spigots with screw-cap fittings and a wooden spigot for use with barrels. Obviously if you have a spigot on your barrel, you don't necessarily have to bottle your wine.

Red Wine

38MM SCREW-CAP SPIGOT

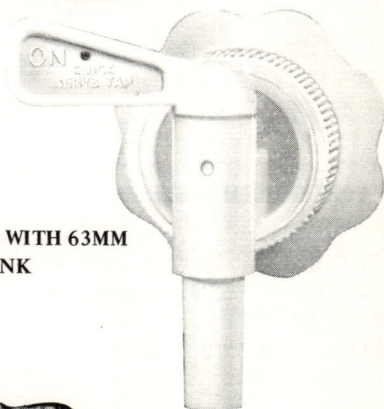

**SPIGOT FOR USE WITH 63MM
WIDE-MOUTH TANK**

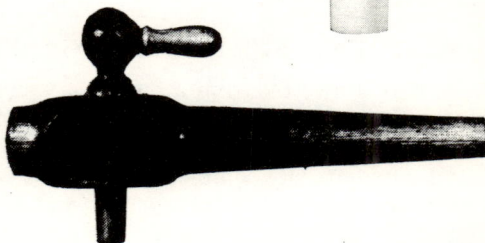

WOODEN SPIGOT FOR BARRELS

51

BARREL MAINTENANCE SUPPLIES

SODA ASH

Soda ash is a very strong caustic soap that will remove all traces of wine residues in barrels, and also will remove the "wood" flavor in new barrels.

SULFUR CANDLE

When burned, this candle will give off sulfur dioxide gas which will kill bacteria and mold. All barrels should receive this treatment before each fermentation. Burn the candle inside the barrel until the oxygen within the barrel is used up. Then tightly stopper the barrel for 24 hrs.

SULFUR STICKS

These sticks serve the same purpose as candles, and are preferred by some.

BARREL BRUSH

This specially-designed winemaker's brush with a 28″ handle is invaluable for cleaning and scrubbing the inside of fermentation vessels. Its long, flexible steel shaft permits you to work around the corners on the inside of a carboy or barrel. The bristles are long and sturdy.

AUTOMATIC SULFUR DIOXIDE GENERATOR

As wine is drawn off from a barrel, a vacuum forms inside that eventually may suck in air and invite contamination. This unusual device responds to the vacuum and automatically combines water with two chemicals in the generator to release sulfur dioxide gas into the barrel to provide a protective blanket for the wine inside.

Red Wine

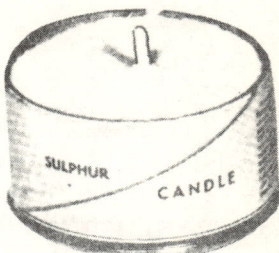

SULFUR CANDLE

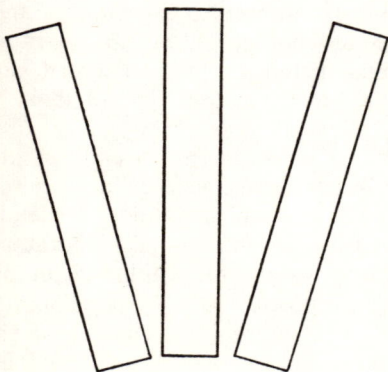

SULFUR STICKS

AUTOMATIC SULFUR DIOXIDE GENERATOR

WINEMAKER'S THERMOMETER

It is important that all cellar work be conducted within a fairly narrow temperature range. Fermentation temperatures should not be allowed to exceed 85°, and aging temperatures should not go below 50° in most cases. This thermometer includes a ring so that it can be lowered into a wine barrel or other type of tank.

MICRO LAB SCALE

Much of the work in a well-run wine cellar requires the accurate measurement of small quantities of chemicals. Here is an inexpensive, yet quality-built laboratory scale that will weigh powders to within .5 gram. Useful for many other purposes.

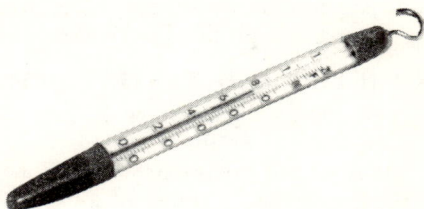

WINEMAKER'S THERMOMETER

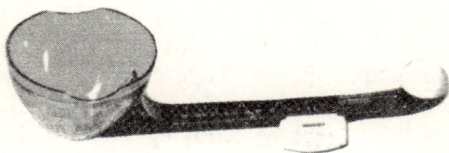

MICRO LAB SCALE

SUGAR TESTING

Just about the most valuable piece of equipment to the winemaker is the hydrometer. It must be used to determine sugar content of the juice, which, in turn, must be correct for proper final alcohol content.

HYDROMETER AND TESTING JAR

The high-quality hydrometer is precision made of blown glass and shows three scales: Brix (% sugar), specific gravity, and potential % alcohol.

The Brix scale has a range of —3% to 38% with .5% graduations that are easy to read. You can determine the amount of sugar to be added by taking a reading of the juice with this hydrometer and referring to the handy conversion table in this book. Additional instructions are generally included with a hydrometer. This particular 10″ hydrometer is packaged in a clear plastic case with a stand that doubles as a test jar for your samples.

OPTICAL SACCHARIMETER

This remarkable scientific instrument quickly, easily, and accurately measures sugar content in a juice. It consists of a metal tube with an adjustable eyepiece and a measuring prism. To use, place a few drops of juice on the prism and hold the instrument up to the sky or a bright ceiling. Looking through the eyepiece, one sees a circle divided into light and dark areas. The eyepiece is adjusted until a sharp edge divides these two areas. This edge crosses a scale which gives you the exact sugar % (Brix) of the juice. (Range is 0-32%.) While the instrument takes the place of a hydrometer or saccharometer, it is especially useful for testing the sugar content of grapes on the vines, thereby indicating the optimum time of harvest.

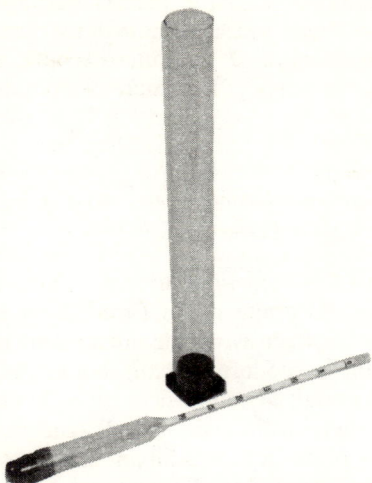

HYDROMETER AND TESTING JAR

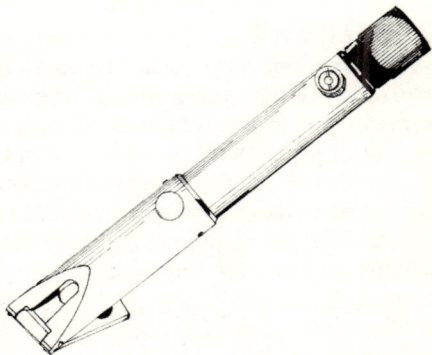

OPTICAL SACCHARIMETER

INVERT SUGAR

In all but the choicest grapes and fruits, sugar content is inadequate and sugar must be added to obtain the optimum alcohol strength. Of course, the added sugar can be regular table sugar (sucrose), but this is not the same as natural grape sugar, which is largely dextrose. The slight difference in chemical composition does tend to show up in the by-products of fermentation. Juice to which invert sugar rather than sucrose has been added will make a better wine.

JUICE STERILIZERS *(Campden Tablets)*

To protect fruit and grape juices (and all equipment that will come in contact with the juices) from wild yeasts, bacteria, and mycoderma aceti, the use of sulfur dioxide in solution is an absolute necessity. A 12-grain tablet of sodium metabisulfite dissolved in a gallon of juice provides 50 parts per million of sulfur dioxide. This concentration is enough to destroy unwanted organisms and yet not affect cultured wine yeasts.

YEAST NUTRIENT

All juices to which sugar has been added need yeast nutrient to provide the yeast with a "balanced diet" so that they will not lose strength as the alcohol content increases during fermentation. To avoid premature cessation of fermentation ("stuck" fermentation) and to assure highest alcohol content, add an 8-grain tablet to the "must" for each pound of sugar added. Useful for restarting a "stuck fermentation."

EQUIPMENT AND SUPPLIES FOR ACID TESTING

The second step in treating the juice is to determine its acid content. This is done by titration against an alkaline solution of known strength, with acid-testing papers, or with a pH meter. California grapes tend to be low in acid content, and it is generally necessary to add acid. Eastern grapes, on the other hand, tend to be quite high in acidity, and it is often desirable to either dilute the juice or treat it with a mild caustic such as calcium carbonate.

TITRATION EQUIPMENT

Titration with a burette is the standard laboratory method for determining acid content. To do this, one simply measures out 10 milliliters of juice into a test tube, and adds to it a few drops of phenolphthalein indicator. (This indicator has the characteristic of being purple in color in an alkaline solution and clear when in an acid solution.) Since all fruit juices are acid, there should be little or no color in the test tube at this point. Now, a standard 10% alkaline solution is slowly added from a calibrated burette into the test solution. The amount of alkaline solution needed to change to purple the color of the liquid in the test tube indicates the acid content of the juice.

The calculation is simply one of multiplying the quantity of alkaline solution by .075 to arrive at the percentage acid content. For example, if it takes 7 milliliters of the 10% alkaline solution to neutralize 10 milliliters of juice, that means that the juice has an acid content of .525% (7 ml. $\times$ .075 = .525%). Now, since we would like the acid content to be about .7% (rather than .525%, as in the example), we will want to add some acid to the juice. If, on the other hand, the acid content had turned out to be over .7%, we would have either diluted the juice with water, or treated it with a weak alkali such as calcium carbonate. While all of this may sound fairly complex, the operation is really rather simple, particularly if the proper equipment is used.

PROFESSIONAL-MODEL TITRATION KIT

This kit contains everything needed to scientifically determine the acid content of your wine. It consists of one laboratory-grade pipette for accurately measuring the wine sample, one precision-made 25-milliliter burette for titrating the normal alkaline solution, a burette stand and clamp, a test tube, 4 ounces of 10% standard alkaline solution, phenolphthalein indicator, and complete instructions including acid-conversion tables.

ECONOMY-MODEL TITRATION KIT

This kit serves the same purpose as the professional model, but uses plunger-syringes instead of the more accurate burette and pipette. While somewhat less accurate, the kit will do an adequate job. It consists of two syringes (one for juice and one for the normal alkaline solution), a 1¼-ounce dispenser bottle of phenolphthalein indicator, 4 ounces of a normal 10% alkaline solution, a test tube, and very complete instructions for determining acid content and computing corrective quantities.

pH METER

This type of meter is the last word in acid-testing equipment. Electrically operated, this pH meter measures acid content to within .001%. It is an extravagance, to be sure, but for the winemaker who enjoys having equipment that will be the very envy of his winemaking friends, this device is practically a necessity.

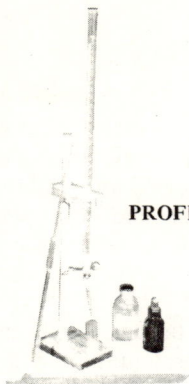

PROFESSIONAL-MODEL TITRATION KIT

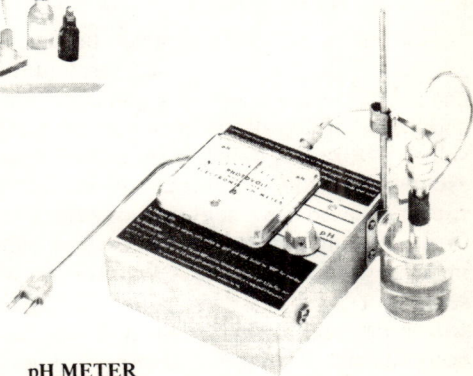

pH METER

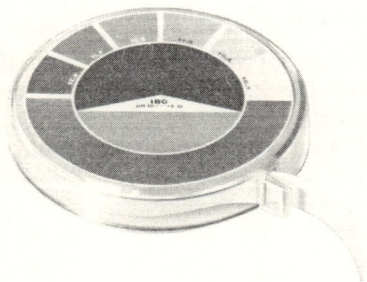

pH PAPERS

pH PAPERS

Fifteen feet of indicator paper, enclosed in a handy dispenser, are sensitized to detect by means of color change comparisons, various levels of acidity within about .2%. This is the easiest and least expensive method of acid detection, but its accuracy is limited.

ACIDS AND NEUTRALIZERS

For juices deficient in acid, tartaric acid should be added to the "must" before fermentation. Citric acid can also be used for this purpose, but preferably it should be added after fermentation rather than before, since it forms soluble iron citrate compounds which are used up during fermentation. Tannic acid is not used for increasing acidity, but rather is mainly an aid in developing proper aging in white wines and endowing the wine with "bite." Without it, white wines will seem flat, characterless, and lacking in "zest." Red wines do not normally need extra tannic acid since there usually is natural tannin in the skins.

For juices with too high an acid content, calcium carbonate can be used to reduce the acidity.

TARTARIC ACID

Each 3.8 grams (approximately 1 teaspoon) per gallon of juice raises the acid content .1%. Up to 7 grams per gallon can be added to the "must." Tartaric acid is available in: 3-ounce packet and 13-ounce bulk.

CITRIC ACID

Each 3.3 grams (approximately 1 teaspoon) per gallon of juice raises the acid content .1%. This is about the maximum amount which can be added without adversely affecting the taste. Citric acid is available in 3-ounce packet and 13-ounce bulk.

TANNIC ACID

About 1 gram per 5 gallons should be added to juices to be used for white wines. This amount does not add significant acidity, but improves aging characteristics. Tannic acid is available in ½-ounce packet.

CALCIUM CARBONATE

Calcium carbonate will combine with excess acid to form insoluble compounds that will settle and can be removed by racking or filtering. 2.5 grams per gallon (approximately 1½ teaspoons) lowers acidity by .1%. This powder is finely divided in laboratory form, and should be added slowly to avoid foaming. If more than 5 grams appears to be needed per gallon, dilution of the "must" with water is recommended. Calcium carbonate is available in 3-ounce packet, 13-ounce bulk.

FERMENTATION LOCKS (*Water-Seal-Valves*)

This is an essential piece of equipment for every winemaker. A fermentation lock allows the carbon dioxide gas generated during fermentation to escape, while preventing air from getting back into the fermentation tank.

WATER-SEAL

This uniquely-designed valve is the preferred choice of winemakers all over the world. It is attractive, foolproof, reliable, rugged, and inexpensive.

BLOWN GLASS WATER-SEAL

These valves, imported from Germany, are like a piece of jewelry. They are handsome, but delicate. A fine gift item for the winemaker who takes pride in the appearance of his cellar.

ANTI-FOAM

This emulsion should be kept handy to retard foaming and consequent overflowing if early fermentation becomes overactive. It will stop foaming very rapidly without affecting the progress of fermentation.

Red Wine

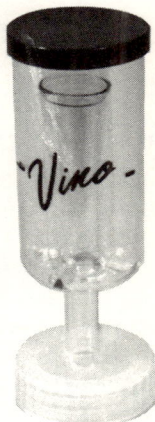

VINO WATER-SEAL

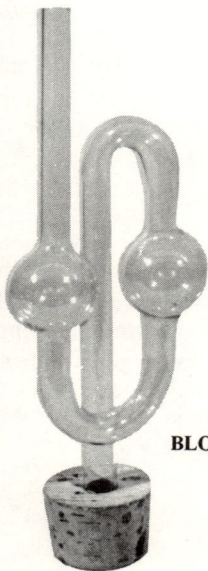

BLOWN GLASS WATER-SEAL

YEAST

ALL-PURPOSE DRY WINE YEAST

For all-around use, this is the finest wine yeast available. Derived from the yeast used to make the great French Burgundy, "Le Montrachet," these cultures will ensure consistently good results. Like all cultured wine yeasts, it is tolerant to mild concentrations of sulfur dioxide, and its value is proven by use in many commercial wineries throughout the U.S. It comes sealed in nitrogen in foil envelopes and has a shelf life of 2 years, if kept in a cool, dry area. Each packet will start up to 5 gallons of wine and includes instructions for starting. All-purpose yeast comes in 1-packet size, 3-packet and 6-packet sizes.

SPECIAL DRY WINE YEASTS

Two special yeasts, Sherry and Champagne, made and packaged like the Montrachet Yeast are available to provide special characteristics and flavor. The Champagne yeast gives a slow, long-lasting fermentation that can continue to work after bottling. The Sherry yeast may create a characteristic "flor." Both are sealed in nitrogen in foil envelopes and have a 2-year shelf life. Each will start up to 5 gallons of wine.

9. Clarifying—*An Overview*—The white of an egg laid by a speckled hen dropped into the wine barrel by the light of a full moon is the ancient ritual by which wine is made crystal clear. Twentieth-century man has tried to be more scientific about it. While sediment and lees are a natural by-product of winemaking, they add nothing to the final enjoyment of the wine. A truly fine wine must be pleasing to the eye as well as to the taste. A "star-bright" wine through which you can see a candle flame without distortion will bring satisfaction to the maker even before it is tasted.

Any stems, seeds, or skins floating in the wine are easily removed by straining. Sediment that has settled to the bottom of the tank or barrel is easily separated by siphoning off the clear wine above. This process, commonly called "racking," may be done one or more times before, during, or after aging. By racking several times during aging, the final clarification may be made easier. Nevertheless, most wines will have some degree of cloudiness even after racking.

The particular treatment used to remove haze depends on the source of the trouble. Most cloudiness is due to the colloidal suspension of fine particles of organic matter or excess acid in crystal form. If the particles are fairly coarse and can be seen with the naked eye, filtration is probably the best way to remove them. (Filtering should be done as rapidly as possible to minimize contact with air, and the use of an anti-oxidant like iso-ascorbic acid is helpful.) If the individual particles are too small to see, various "fining" agents must be used. Protein in various forms, Sparkolloid™ or gelatin, will tend to envelop the colloids and cause them to settle. In more persistent cases, a non-organic fining agent like bentonite should be used. Stubborn haze may require both of these treatments plus further filtration. Unfortunately, this complete treatment is somewhat harsh on the wine, and it may be necessary to restore some of the tannin that fining takes away. Tannin is necessary for proper maturing of the wine.

If all these methods fail, the last resort is activated charcoal. Unfortunately, this will tend to remove color and flavor as well. Once again, modern chemistry comes to the rescue of the winemaker, and it is possible to add back artificial color and flavorings. Actually, some very delightful effects can be achieved with artificial flavors, and experiments with orange, peach, strawberry, and many other flavors may turn what might have been a disappointment into a triumph.

Racking—The next operation is "racking" or separating the wine juice from the bottom deposit (called "lees") of your container.

The easiest method of separating the two is to draw off the juice from the container into another container by using a siphon. For this purpose any flexible tubing will suffice, but it is a great convenience to have an automatic siphon which is started by squeezing the siphon-pump's bellows. Automatic siphons also have a pressure valve that is handy for bottling. An example of a typical automatic siphon is *illustrated on page 71*.

Several days before you start racking, lift the wine-holding container to a higher elevation such as a kitchen stool or chair or table. When moving the container, use care so that you do not stir up the wine juice sediment. Insert one end of the siphon-pump or plastic tube into this container and insert the other end into a second empty container that is lower in elevation than the first container. Start siphoning and continue until all the clear wine has been transferred to the second container. Be sure to stop the siphon before the lees are transferred.

If, after racking, your wine continues to be cloudy, you can make it clearer by adding a special clarifying agent. Common clarifying agents are bentonite and Sparkolloid™. Both are available from winemaking supply dealers in powder or tablet forms. Tablets are generally formulated in the correct dosage to treat a gallon of wine. You can make up a clarifying solution by dissolving the appropriate number of clarifier tablets in a minimum amount of hot water. Then, pour equal portions of your clarifier agent into each container of your wine. Within three days you will note a fine sediment forming on the bottom of the container. The wine on top should be clear. Wine treated in this manner can then be drawn off by opening the barrel spigot, or by siphoning it off into another container, leaving the sediment behind.

Balancing—You are now ready for your final steps before bottling. Since it is entirely possible that you have fermented your wine to an absolutely dry condition, you may wish for a little sweetness to satisfy your taste buds. This means you need to add a modicum of sugar. In adding the sugar, the maximum amount is two ounces per gallon. The exact amount is a matter of personal preference. Keep in mind that sugar will not necessarily make your wine more pleasing to the taste.

However, a word of caution. By adding sugar, it is entirely possible that fermentation will start all over again, resulting in broken bottles and blown corks. Therefore, it is necessary to add a preservative to prevent further fermentation. Common preservatives are ascorbic acid and potassium sorbate. Again, these chemicals are available in tablet form so that 1 tablet per gallon is a correct dosage.

SIPHONING EQUIPMENT

"Racking" is the process of removing the clear wine from the spent yeast and other insoluble particles (called "lees") which, at the end of fermentation, have settled to the bottom of the fermenting tank or barrel. It is an exceedingly simple procedure, but an important one. Wine which is not racked generally develops the musty flavor of decomposed yeast. While there are various types of siphons available, all of them do essentially the same job—that of transferring the clear liquid from one container to another. The differences are in ease of operation and in the speed with which they transfer the wine.

AUTOMATIC SIPHON

This siphon was designed with the needs in mind of the winemaker who is very particular about equipment. It is equipped with a stop-peg that prevents the end of the siphon tube from touching the bottom of the tank and picking up sediment. It has a plastic bellows with which siphoning action is started, and the faucet has an automatic trigger shut-off for easy bottling. This siphon tube is a 4-foot length of laboratory-grade vinyl tubing with an inside diameter of ½″. With this, a maximum flow rate of more than one gallon per minute can be achieved.

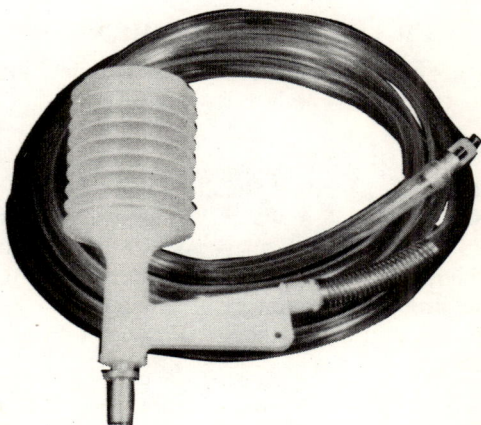

AUTOMATIC SIPHON

FILTRATION EQUIPMENT

For wines with visible, suspended particles, filtration is the most practical method of removal.

FILTER KIT

This kit is designed especially for the home wine-maker. Consisting of a water vacuum pump (aspirator), a 4″-diameter Buchner-type vacuum funnel, a 1-qt. receiving jar, and a supply of filter paper, it minimizes the amount of contact the wine has with air. Pump, funnel, and jar are heavy-duty polyethylene, and easily cleaned.

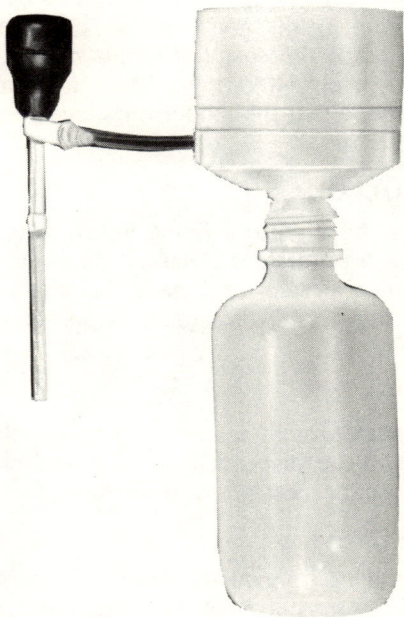

FILTER KIT

FINING AGENTS

Below is listed a series of fining agents that wi cause finely divided particles, too small to be filterec to either coalesce so that they can be filtered or settl so that they can be separated by siphoning. These finin or clarifying agents are listed in order of increasin strength. Since the stronger agents can, if used incor rectly, adversely affect wine flavor and/or color, it i recommended that the milder ones, such as sparkolloic be tried first.

SPARKOLLOID ™

This is the preferred fining agent and the one tha should be tried first. It is largely protein, but include several mineral salts to enhance its effectiveness. On 10-grain tablet or ¼ teaspoon of powder treats a gal lon of wine.

GELATIN

This pure protein material when dissolved in win will envelop the suspended particles and cause them t settle. It clears most types of haziness.

BENTONITE

This is a non-organic material in combination witl a special porous clay that will trap and cause to settl very stubborn colloids and haze particles. Sprinkl about 3 grams (approx. 1 teaspoon) per gallon of wine and allow time to settle.

ACTIVATED CHARCOAL

This is a "last resort" method. It is the strongest of all fining agents. If this does not clear your wine, there is nothing more that can be done for it. Use no more than 2-grams per gallon for this purpose. Also useful for removing excess color and unwanted flavors.

PECTIC ENZYME

This is the same material suggested for use prior to pressing the fruit. If it was not used at that time, how-ever, it can be used to clarify the wine before bottling. It works by breaking down the bonds of pectin in sus-pended particles. To use, dissolve two 8-grain tablets or about ¼ teaspoon of powder per gallon of wine and allow to stand for 3 hours.

RED WINE COLORING

If heavy use of fining agents has been employed in clarification, the color of the wine may be affected. Per-haps, too, the color was not satisfactory in the first place. In either event, this red-wine coloring will pro-vide a rich, red-wine color without affecting the flavor. Each ½-oz. packet will color 5 to 10 gallons.

VINOMETER

This compact, precision-made scientific instrument is ideal for checking the alcohol content of finished wine. Consisting of a calibrated glass capillary tube with a small thistle-shaped funnel, the instrument works on the principle of differences in surface tension of various concentrations of alcohol. To use, the tube is filled through the funnel with a few drops of wine and then inverted. The wine runs slowly down the tube and stops at a point on the scale equal to the percentage of alcohol in the wine. Calibrated from 0 to 25% alcohol in easy-to-read graduations. Most accurate with dry wines at room temperature.

WINE THIEF

This device provides a simple way of drawing samples from a barrel or tank to determine if the wine is clear enough to avoid further treatment. It is also useful for taking samples to see if further aging is required. "Steal" a little wine to taste or test with this wine thief.

WINE STABILIZER-PRESERVATIVE
(*Iso-Ascorbic Acid*)

Bitterness in a finished wine is often due to excessive exposure to air. The addition of small quantities of this anti-oxidant before bottling will protect the wine against oxidation and loss of flavor or color. Wine treated with this chemical need not be consumed immediately upon opening the bottle. A half-consumed bottle of wine can be stored for days without fear of spoilage. One gram treats about 2½ gallons of wine; ½ ounce treats 35 gallons.

Red Wine

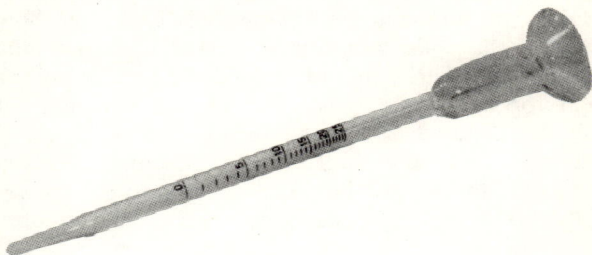

VINOMETER

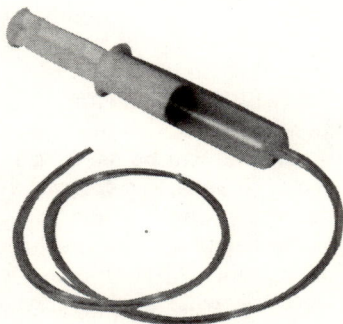

WINE THIEF

10. Bottling—Bottling is the culmination of the winemaking process. For months the winemaker has awaited this moment. He has carefully extracted the essence of the fruit, scientifically tested it for sweetness and acidity, nourished and created the proper environment for the young yeast cells to perform their vital task, brilliantly clarified the resultant liquor, and patiently awaited the end results of the chemical processes of aging. At long last, the time has come to put the wine in the bottle and lay it down to sleep its final hours to maturity.

While the actual process of bottling is a simple one, it is perhaps the most pleasant in the entire winemaking operation. Tasting is, of course, one of its primary attractions. This is the "moment of truth" when the winemaker receives his final report card. Is the wine dry or sweet? What about its flavor? Does the wine have body, or is it thin? What about its acidity? Does it taste sharp, or is it mellow?

Since the serving of wine is highly steeped in tradition, the true connoisseur will want the proper showcase for his wine. Burgundy-style bottles with their long, graceful necks will be used for burgundies, rosés, moselles, and vermouths. Bordeaux-style bottles, the ones with "shoulders", will be used for bordeaux wines, sauternes, clarets, chiantis, and sherries. It is unthinkable that sparkling wines would come any way but in a champagne bottle complete with mushroom corks, wire hood, and foil capsule. All bottles, of course, will be tinted to protect the wine against daylight. This is of particular importance for red wines which may deteriorate quickly upon exposure to light.

Although there are traditions governing the shape and color of wine bottles, in reality, ginger ale, other soft drinks, or even beer bottles are perfectly utilitarian.

Red Wine

Good wine bottles are more expensive than most people realize, especially when purchased in small quantities with additional freight charges. However, these bottles can be reused almost indefinitely, if properly cleaned each time. (Ecologists cheer!)

Regardless of the source or age of your bottles, during bottling they must be absolutely free of contamination. Cleanliness is essential. While new bottles may easily be rinsed with hot water, used ones will require more extensive cleaning and should be thoroughly washed with hot, soapy water and brushed inside with a bottle brush. They should be "squeaky" clean. For the absolute in cleanliness, you can prepare a rinsing solution by dissolving four bisulfite tablets in a cup of water and swishing it around in each bottle. It is possible to transfer this solution from one bottle to another by means of a funnel. Drain the bottles thoroughly. Never use bottles that have even a trace of soap or detergent remaining, since soapy-flavored wine is as yet unpopular.

The bottling itself can be simplified even more with the use of special filling equipment. The automatic siphon described in connection with clarifying is very helpful. Its use reduces the chance of loss of the precious fluid and also speeds up the operation, thus reducing the possibility of oxidizing the wine. In this connection, the use of a preservative, like ascorbic acid, will help prevent possible deterioration of the wine in the bottle, as well as prevent any further fermentation.

Once the bottles are filled, they must be corked or capped. While screw caps are simpler to use, corking is not only more romantic, but permits the wine to breathe, thus providing continued aging in the bottle. The use of foil capsules on top of the corks will dress up the bottle even more.

A wine without a label is like an unsigned painting and, if the winemaker is truly proud of his accomplishment, he will personally want to label it. Not only will an attractive label enhance the appearance of the bottle, but it will serve as a good record of the type of wine and the vintage year. Carrying this one step farther, many winemakers find it quite helpful to maintain a notebook of their winemaking activities, indicating in it all the pertinent facts regarding each bottle of wine produced—type of fruit, date of harvest, acidity and sugar content before amelioration, fermentation time, etc. By documenting all this information, the winemaker not only can repeat his successes, but can also profit from his mistakes.

WINE BOTTLES

Bottling your wine in the proper bottle certainly enhances its appeal. Green, flint glass bottles are available in the following types:

BURGUNDY STYLE

1/5 gallon, champagne-green.

BORDEAUX STYLE

1/5 gallon, champagne-green.

CHAMPAGNE

1/5 gallon, extra-heavy champagne-green glass, lip for crown cap, 26mm neck finish for plastic stopper.

Red Wine

BURGUNDY STYLE

BORDEAUX STYLE

CHAMPAGNE STYLE

BOTTLE FILLERS

Operating with siphon action, these bottle fillers virtually eliminate loss of wine due to spillage. Incorporating a patented self-closing valve, these fillers make it unnecessary to manually open and close the tap. When pressed onto the neck of a bottle to be filled, the spring-loaded nozzle valve automatically closes the valve, shutting off the liquid flow. Speed of flow can be regulated from one gallon per minute on down to a trickle.

BOTTLE BRUSH (*Mechanical*)

It is imperative that all bottles be absolutely clean before bottling the wine. This mechanical revolving brush performs the task of bottle cleaning without fatigue and without risk of bottle breakage. As the handle is drawn up and down, the brush whirls around very rapidly within the bottle. It does an efficient and thorough job of scouring the interior surface of the bottle, all within a few seconds.

BOTTLE BRUSH (*Manual*)

A 7″ long, 3″ wide horsehair brush with a 17″ flexible steel rod. Fits all wine bottles.

JET RINSER

Here is another machine which takes all the mess and tedium out of bottle washing. This unit attaches to a standard, threaded, laundry-tub (¾″ N.P.T.) faucet. When a bottle is pressed onto the top of the valve, a fine, powerful jet is directed up into the bottle.

Red Wine

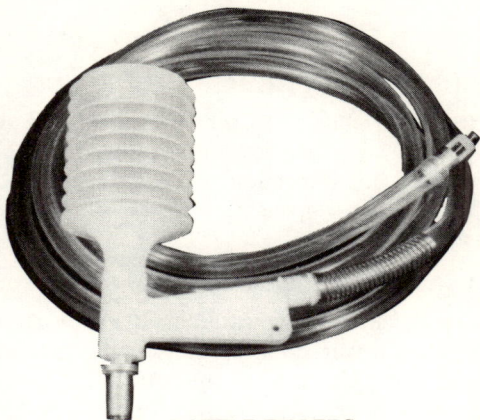

BOTTLE FILLERS

BOTTLE BRUSH (MECHANICAL)

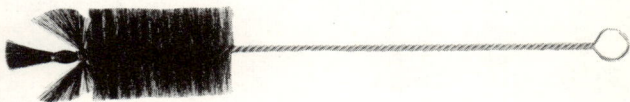

BOTTLE BRUSH (MANUAL)

JET RINSER

CHAMPAGNE STOPPERS

These reusable, plastic closures are now used almost exclusively by U.S. wineries in corking their champagnes and sparkling burgundies. Their ridged construction makes it nearly impossible for the champagne to lose its sparkle.

CHAMPAGNE WIRE HOODS

For use with champagne stoppers, these wire hoods prevent closures from popping out, regardless of the gas pressure. They also add to the attractiveness of the finished product.

FOIL CAPSULES

Nothing quite finishes off the appearance of a wine or champagne bottle like a foil capsule. The aluminum capsules are very neat and can be applied with a simple rubber crimping ring. The lead capsules have a more expensive, professional look, but are somewhat more difficult to apply. They are available in red or gold-color lead foil, red aluminum foil, or gold-color Special Champagne foil.

CRIMPING RUBBER

A simple mechanism for applying aluminum capsules.

CAPSULER

An ingenious tool for easily applying lead and aluminum capsules to wine bottles.

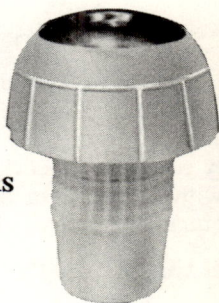

CHAMPAGNE STOPPERS

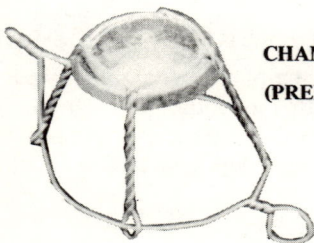

**CHAMPAGNE WIRE HOODS
(PREMIUM GRADE WITH PLAQUES)**

CAPSULER

CORKING MACHINES

The use of any of these three corking machines will provide a real assist—particularly if you are bottling two or more gallons at a time. The bench model quickly and simply corks a considerable number of bottles with a minimum of effort. The two hand models are equally effective, although somewhat slower.

HAMMER-TYPE HAND CORKER

Compresses the cork, allowing it to be tapped into the bottle. Constructed of rugged aluminum.

LEVER-TYPE HAND CORKER

Works on the same principle, but employs lever action to force the cork into the bottle. The length of the piston can be adjusted so that a cork can be inserted into a bottle to any desired depth. Made of solid aluminum.

BENCH-MODEL CORKER

This unique machine, weighing only 11 pounds, makes corking fast and foolproof. Suitable for all kinds of bottles from standard fifths to champagne magnums. Also has an attachment which converts it into a crown capper. Made of solid bronze, this is a must for the high-volume winemaker.

CROWN CAPPER

For those who wish to bottle their wines in ginger-ale or similar-type soda bottles, this crown capper makes the capping job exceedingly fast, effective, and inexpensive.

HAMMER-TYPE HAND CORKER

LEVER-TYPE HAND CORKER

BENCH-TYPE CORKER   **CROWN CAPPER**

WINE LABELS

The ultimate finishing touch to your wine is an at
tractive label that creates a personalized image of th
care and quality that you have put into your win
These labels are available in packages of one doze
four dozen or ten dozen.

SPECIAL LABELS

Part Three:

White Wine

11. Crushing and Pressing—The discussion in the previous six chapters was primarily devoted to making red wines. In this section of the book, the same basic winemaking steps will be repeated along with suggestions that are pertinent to white wine only. We will also point out the basic differences involved in processing red and white wines.

Although dark grapes can be used to make both red and white wines, light grapes are preferable for white wines. When making white wines, the grape skins are not included in the fermentation process. Generally speaking, the grape that can be used most effectively to make white wines has a skin that slips off easily!

The grapes of the Northern states that may be used to make white wine include the Catawba which has a distinctive, tasty, tart flavor. The Niagara, a cousin to the Concord grape, is plentiful but is not an ideal wine grape since it is high in acid and low in sugar. The French hybrid grapes, including Seyve-Villard #5276, Ravat Blanc, Riesling and Pinot Chardonnay, are excellent white wine grapes but are not always available.

In the Western states, the best of the white grapes are Pinot Chardonnay, Johannisburg Riesling and Pinot Blanc. Other excellent varieties include French Columbard, Sauvignon Blanc and Gewurztraminer. Common grapes used extensively in white winemaking include Muscats, Sultanas, Thompsons, Malagas and Palominos.

In the Southern states, a native variety that makes a good white wine is the Scuppernong.

In making white wine, keep in mind that you don't use the skins, and they should not be allowed to come in contact at any time with the fermenting juice. To prevent contact, crush and immediately press the grapes. Do not remove the stems since they will aid in crushing and pressing and will be eliminated during pressing, anyway.

The same identical process is used to crush grapes for white and red wine. The method of pressing depends on the amount of wine you plan to make. As we mentioned previously, a bushel of grapes weighing 50 lbs., will yield roughly 50 gallons of juice. If you intend to make your legal maximum of 200 gallons of wine, you will probably decide to use a high capacity "basket-type" press. For lesser quantities, one of the smaller "basket-type" presses will prove to be more than adequate. For very small quantities (one to four bushels of grapes), after crushing them with a potato masher, or a wooden two-by-four, or your hands, etc., you can press the crushed grapes by placing them in a cheesecloth or special pressing bag. Then, squeeze the juice out by thoroughly wringing out the bag. Another possibility is to hang the bag from a board, place it over a bucket and let the juice drain out overnight.

12. Treating the Juice—After crushing and immediately pressing, the next step is to siphon off a pint of grape juice and test the sample for sugar content. To test for sugar, use the same steps as discussed in the red wine section. The grapes that make the best white wines generally have a sugar content of about 22° on the Brix scale. This reading is considered by most experts to be an ideal Brix level for making white wine. As with red wines, it may be necessary to add sugar to the grape juice to bring it up to the 22° level. When adding sugar, use the granulated variety and "gently stir" it into the juice until it becomes completely dissolved.

We used the word "siphon" in drawing off a sample and we feel this word should be emphasized. Do not pour or slosh the juice from one container to another, and handle the container as little as possible. If it is handled too frequently, the juice may oxidize and turn to a brownish color. Can you imagine anything worse than serving your boss' wife a brownish-white wine with her lobster!

For your convenience and assistance in determining the right amount of additional sugar to bring the juice's Brix reading up to 22°, we have prepared the following chart.

Addition of sugar—Calculated on basis that .125 pounds of sugar per gallon will raise Balling 1°.

percent sugar in must	*add sugar per gallons*				
	pounds		*ounces*		*cups*
22	.00		.00		.00
21	.13	or	2.00	or	.25
20	.25	or	4.00	or	.50
19	.38	or	6.00	or	.75
18	.50	or	8.00	or	1.00
17	.63	or	10.00	or	1.25
16	.75	or	12.00	or	1.50
15	.88	or	14.00	or	1.75
14	1.00	or	16.00	or	2.00
13	1.13	or	18.00	or	2.25
12	1.25	or	20.00	or	2.50
11	1.38	or	22.00	or	2.75
10	1.50	or	24.00	or	3.00
9	1.63	or	26.00	or	3.25
8	1.75	or	28.00	or	3.50
7	1.88	or	30.00	or	3.75
6	2.00	or	32.00	or	4.00
5	2.13	or	34.00	or	4.25
4	2.25	or	36.00	or	4.50
3	2.38	or	38.00	or	4.75
2	2.50	or	40.00	or	5.00
1	2.63	or	42.00	or	5.25
0	2.75	or	44.00	or	5.50

The second step in making white wine is the same as in red wine—check your juice for acidity. This is *discussed on page 29*. Juice that is too high in acid tends to be sharp and never attains real smoothness, but retains an unwanted, bitter green taste. As a general rule, Eastern grapes tend to be too high in acid, while those grapes grown in our Western states tend to be too low. Good wine has an acid reading that falls between .70 percent and 1.00. If the acid reading of your juice falls below .70 percent, add tartaric acid, or some similar acid blend to bring the acid level up to .70 percent.

13. Fermenting—Fermentation will start about 1 to 1½ days after you have added the wine yeast to the grape juice, although it is entirely possible that it may take slightly longer. However, relax! Unless there is a preservative in the juice, fermentation is guaranteed to take place. Bubbles of foam popping up around the outside edges of the juice are its first evidence. These bubbles will then turn into a rolling and frothing action that increases in intensity as the yeast starts to grow and do its work.

Proper temperature control is especially important during fermentation. 65°F is considered to be ideal, and, under no conditions should it be permitted to drop below 60°F or rise much above 75°F.

It is entirely possible that highly active foaming will take place during fermentation. To reduce this condition, use an anti-foaming agent that reduces surface tension and limits foaming.

If you find that even the anti-foaming agent is unable to control the violent frothing, transfer some of the juice into another container. Another possibility is to fill your plastic container only two-thirds full for the primary fermentation. When the fermentation and subsequent foaming start to slow down, fill the container with juice until there is only two or three inches between the bottom of the cork and the liquid's top.

To prevent blown corks and irate wives, place a loose fitting plug on the container while violent fermentation is taking place.

Once the violent frothing stops, place a water seal on the container. Complete fermentation may require anywhere from a few weeks to a month or more. Temperature has a great deal to do with the amount of time that is required. When no more bubbles appear in the water seal (fermentation lock), test the sugar content to determine how completely the sugar has been used up. Again, use either a hydrometer, or conduct a simple sugar test by dipping a diabetic test tape into the wine and checking the color of this tape against the color that is printed on the box. If, for example, the color of the tape remains yellow, there is no sugar left and your wine is completely dry. If you have too much sugar, test it with your hydrometer. For further information about testing, check the discussion in the red wine chapter.

If there is too much sugar in your wine at this time, you should become concerned since you may have a stuck wine, or a yeast strain that is intolerant to alcohol at only the 12% level.

If you find your wine stuck, it means fermentation has stopped before it should have. You must take immediate action! If, on the other hand, your hydrometer reading indicates there is little or no sugar in the wine (specific gravity is below 1.00), the wine hasn't stopped fermenting or become stuck, but has merely run out of sugar.

You should also take a temperature reading, as there is a strong possibility you have stored your container in a place that is so cold that the yeast is unable to react. If this is the case, merely move the container to a warmer room.

SUBSCRIBE TO THE "VINO NEWSLETTER"

Mail this card with **$1.00** for 4 quarterly issues of the "VINO NEWSLETTER," the authoritative and timely publication that keeps you abreast of new products, new winemaking recipes, and activities and discoveries of home winemakers around the world. Enclosed is my $1.00. Start my subscription at once.

Name _____

Address _____ Apt. No. _____

State _____ Zip Code _____

To: **VINO CORPORATION**

BOX 7498

ROCHESTER, NY 14615

If this isn't the problem, try adding more grape juice, yeast and yeast nutrient to the stuck wine, or blending it with an actively fermenting wine being made in another container. You can also dilute the stuck wine with sugar water having a 22° reading on the Brix scale. The needed proportions here are three parts sugar water to ten parts wine. Finally as a last resort, aerate the wine at least three times a day by stirring and splashing the wine. This is not recommended except as a last ditch effort since air is the unholy destroyer of juice, must, and even finished wine. White wine is especially endangered since, when it is subjected to air, it oxidizes to an offensive brown color. To keep down oxidation, therefore, use metabisulfite throughout your winemaking process.

14. Clarifying — *Racking* — When fermentation stops completely, fill your plastic container to within one inch from the top with a finished white wine. After the wine clears, it is ready for racking.

However, before racking, it is important that the wine has an adequate sulfur dioxide content. Sulfur dioxide is particularly important in white wine because oxidation must be prevented and sulfur dioxide helps the wine keep its delicate flavor and bouquet. If you know or suspect that there is not enough SO_2 to preserve the wine, you can raise the sulfur dioxide content by dissolving ½ Campden tablet per gallon, or by adding ½ teaspoon of the same stock solution we discussed under making red wines. When adding sulfur dioxide, however, place it in an empty plastic container or glass carboy and then siphon the wine on top of it. A sulfur dioxide content of 50 parts per million cannot be detected by taste, yet is enough to protect the wine. A simple test for SO_2 content is taste. A few taste tests with varying dosages of Campden tablets can indicate if too much SO_2 is present.

Racking is basically the same procedure that we discussed before. Again, do not move the container of wine any more than is absolutely necessary. After allowing the wine to settle for a few days, insert a siphon tube to approximately the middle of the plastic container. Place the other end of the tube on the bottom of the transfer container to prevent aeration and allow a more complete mixing of wine and sulfur dioxide solution previously placed in the empty container.

White wine may require several rackings. Keep in mind the fewer times you must rack to attain a clear wine, the greater are your chances to prevent oxidation. Oxidation may creep in after two rackings, so if you continue to have unclear wine after two rackings, it is advisable to use a fining agent. Fining wine means adding an ingredient that makes the haze and cloudiness in your wine settle to the bottom of the tank. A great many fining agents can be used, but two of the better ones are Sparkolloid™ or bentonite. These are discussed in the chapter on making red wines.

After adding the fining agent, allow the wine to settle for three days or more and then rack again. This should leave the wine clear and bright.

Then, fill the container to within 1″ from the top with a finished wine. It is now time to stabilize.

Stabilizing—For stabilization, keep your wine cold to help precipitate the tartrate. This will give your wine a smoother taste and eliminate the chance of crystals that can form on the bottom of bottled white wine.

For a discussion of stabilization, refer to the chapter on red wines. White wines' stabilization differs slightly from red wine as white wines should be kept in cold storage conditions of about 35°F for approximately 14 days.

Balancing—Balance a white wine the same as you would a red.

Part Four:

Additional Grape Wines

15. Rosé—*Selecting the Ingredients*—Excellent commercial rosé wines can be made from such grape strains as Tavels, Grenache and Gamay. However, the home winemaker can make excellent rosé wine by processing the same red-fleshed grapes that are normally used to make red wines. It is also possible to make a blend of red and white wines.

***Treating the Juice*—**Rosé wines attain their pink color by the skins and juices remaining together for a short period of time. The necessary time might be a matter of hours or days. Large commercial wineries attain a rosé by crushing the grapes and then allowing the juice and skins to ferment together briefly before pressing; or, by crushing and pressing the grapes immediately and then pouring the pressed juice back into the vats that contain the skins. They then allow the juice and skins to ferment a sufficiently long time so that the juice extracts a pink color.

Of these two methods, the first method requires long years of experience and is the sole reserve of commercial wineries. The home winemaker can use the second method as he can more easily determine the juice's color. However, judging the color does require both skill and judgment so that the beginner basically must learn by trial and error.

Fermenting, aging, bottling procedures, etc., follow the same steps as in making red wines.

16. Champagne, Cold Duck—and Other Sparkling Wines—Sparkling wines are made in two basic ways: (1) by bottling the wine before fermentation is complete, or (2) by conducting a second fermentation by adding sugar or unfermented juice to an existing wine. The second approach is preferred.

There are basically four types of sparkling wines. These are champagne, Sparkling Burgundy, Sparkling Rosé, and Cold Duck (which is a popular new combination of champagne and Sparkling Burgundy). The familiar white champagnes predominate and, in making it, the importance of selecting a choice white wine must be emphasized. It is a sheer waste of time, money and energy to even attempt to make a good quality white champagne from a poorly-made table wine. It isn't in the cards. The only way to ensure quality is by the initial proper selection of grapes to process into white dinner wine. Some of the more prominent white table wine grapes include Pinot Chardonnay, Elvira, Seibel No. 5279, Seyve-Villard No. 12375, Seyve-Villard No. 5276 and last but by no means least—the Delaware, which is considered by many experts to be the finest champagne grape in the world.

In developing Sparkling Burgundy, the Foch grape is highly regarded. It is first fermented into a fine red Burgundy which is then refermented in the bottle.

Excellent champagne also may be made by blending several wines together. One combination that has proved to be successful is 50% Delaware grape wine, 35% Seyval Blanc and 15% Catawba. Other varieties of grapes that can be blended to yield excellent champagnes include Dutchess, White Riesling, Pinot Blanc and Pinot Chardonnay. Due to their acidity and tannin content, grapes grown in the eastern United States are considered to be among the finest of champagne grapes.

Another important factor that must be considered when choosing a white wine to be made into champagne is its clarification and stabilization. The wine should be light in color, ideally, a light yellow, or almost straw in color. The alcoholic content should be no higher than 10%. 11% is considered to be the absolute maximum since wine with an alcoholic content greater than 11% may not ferment a second time. This bottle fermentation is called "referment." The original white wine must have a sugar content of about 20° on the Brix scale to obtain such a low alcoholic content in the finished product.

A fine champagne must develop a "bite" that we all expect and enjoy when sipping. The bubbly effect and "bite" will be enhanced if the original white wine is sufficiently acid. An ideal acidity range is considered to be between .70-.75%. The white wine that will be made into champagne should include tannin to insure good clarification before refermenting and to guard against later cloudiness. Therefore, add tannic acid, if necessary, when making the initial white table wine. As already mentioned, tannin provides that "puckery" sensation one gets when drinking wine. Since white wines are generally quite low in tannic acid, add tannin at the rate of about 1 gram per 5 gallons of wine.

The first step in making champagne from either a fermenting wine or from an existing white wine is to determine the sugar concentration. The wine should contain between 2.5 and 5.0% sugar to achieve good champagne results. In checking for sugar, the following rules of thumb should be kept in mind. If the (grape) juice is 24% sugar at the start of fermentation, (specific gravity of 1.100), when the specific gravity drops to 1.005, the sugar is down to 5% (even though the hydrometer indicates about 1.4% because the alcohol content has gone from 0% to 11%). If the juice is 20% sugar to start (s.g., 1.081), when s.g. drops to 1.009, the sugar content is 5%, although the hydrometer indicates 2.5%. If the juice is 10% to start (s.g., 1.038), when s.g. gets to 1.012, it is 5% sugar, although the hydrometer indicates 3.3%.

If your wine is clear and you wish to avoid the trouble of a second fermentation, you may simply bottle the wine when the sugar content gets down to 2.5 to 5.0% sugar. If the sugar is fermented to below 2.5% and the wine is 10%-11% alcohol, it will be necessary to add enough sugar to get back up to 5%. To do this you should prepare a sugar syrup solution that you will shortly add to the white wine. This syrup should be composed of one part water (or wine) and two parts sugar. You must know exactly how much sugar (in ounces) you are adding to the solution in order to arrive at an accurate measurement. Each ounce of solution will contain ⅔ ounce of sugar.

In either event, the table below will tell you approximately how much sugar to add according to the % already in the wine:

Sugar in Wine	Sugar to be added per gallon
0%	12 teaspoons
.25%	11 teaspoons
.50%	8 teaspoons
.75%	7 teaspoons
1.00%	5 teaspoons
1.25%	2½ teaspoons
1.50%	1 teaspoon
1.75%	none

Be extremely accurate in adding sugar since the bottle may explode during fermentation if too much sugar is added. On the other hand, if less sugar is added than required, there won't be enough carbon dioxide to finish the wine at a later date.

The next step is to add a special fermenting yeast to the container. This yeast is aptly called, "champagne yeast." Then, add either the sugar syrup or the plain sugar.

Now, add a yeast nutrient to aid the fermentation. The approximate proportion is 2 to 5 grams of nutrient per 5 gallons of wine.

It is now time to siphon the wine into champagne bottles. (Heavy duty champagne bottles must be used to avoid breakage. Also, they must be clean.) Fill the bottles to within 1″ to 2″ from the lip. As each bottle is filled, cap it temporarily with a crown, such as a beer bottle cap.

Note that when you first siphon the wine from the primary fermenting container into the champagne bottles, be certain the yeast cells remain with the wine and don't remain behind. Otherwise, the wine will not ferment in the bottle. To avoid this problem, gently stir the wine with a clean rod (preferably of glass) between filling every six or seven bottles. This stirring will help keep the yeast suspended in the juice.

In selecting champagne bottles, be very quality conscious. Remember that these bottles must withstand tremendous pressure during fermentation. Do not use anything other than champagne bottles for fermentation since champagne bottles are specifically designed to withstand tremendous pressure. For example, a new champagne bottle can withstand pressures of better than 200 pounds per square inch. In actual practice, however, a bottle is seldom required to withstand such pressure. Furthermore, some people believe that second-hand champagne bottles have lost some of their strength in their first go-around, and, therefore, are unable to withstand the same pressures that a new bottle can.

Instead of capping your champagne bottle, you may also use a plastic champagne cork purchasable from most wine supply houses. After inserting this cork into the bottle, you will need to fasten it to the bottle neck securely with special wiring.

Once the bottles are filled, place them on their sides in your cellar. Select an area where a room temperature of about 60°F can be maintained.

The secondary fermentation should take between two to three weeks to complete. During this time, take every possible precaution to avoid personal injury in handling the bottles. Remember that fermentation exerts tremendous pressures within these bottles. When working with the wine during this time, wear a face shield and a pair of ski gloves for your own safety.

The bottled wine should rest for at least one year. If you wish, during this period, you may construct a special storage bin to hold the bottles. Such a storage system is called a tierage. As the bottles lie in repose, a mysterious process will take place in which champagne evolves from the wine. A possible scientific explanation is that, as the yeast cells die, their cellular walls dissolve releasing protoplasm. This protoplasm gives the wine its yeasty or champagne-like flavor.

After the wine has rested in the bottles for one year, an optional next step is to remove the sediment that has formed from the dead yeast cells. To remove this sediment, place the bottles on an incline with their necks at the lower end. Better yet, construct a special rack that permits the bottles to be stored neck down at a 70° angle. Then, the sediment may be removed by a process called "riddling." Riddling is accomplished by removing each bottle from its specially constructed rack, giving it a quarter-clockwise turn and dropping it back into its resting place with a gentle thump. This gentle thump causes sediment to slide down the inside surface of the bottle to the neck. Champagne bottles should be lifted and turned (riddled) about two times a day for about three weeks. You should also "candle" the bottles to determine if the sediment has settled. To candle, hold a light behind each bottle to determine clarity.

When riddling is complete and the sediment has flowed into the neck, we are ready for "disgorging." The best way to disgorge is to first chill the bottles by storing in a cold place. When chilling, keep the bottles in a neck-down position, so that the sediment doesn't drift back into the wine. A beer or soft drink case makes an ideal container to use to keep the bottles in this position.

After chilling (ideally at 40°F), a brine composed of coarse salt and chipped ice should be prepared and placed in a tub. Then, put the neck of the chilled bottles into this solution to about 1" to 1½" in depth. Within a half to a full hour, the wine and the sediment in the neck will freeze into a plug. Once the neck is frozen, remove the bottle and place the neck into a pan of warm water for a few seconds. This will help to loosen the frozen neck plug. Then, holding the bottle neck up at a 45° angle, remove the cap with a bottle opener. POW! When the "blow off" occurs, raise the champagne bottle upright to prevent the loss of any wine. (If you used a plastic champagne cork instead of a bottle cap, remove the wire holding the cork and twist off the cork.)

The last step in making champagne is to top off each bottle with a brandy and sugar mixture. To prepare the brandy solution, blend approximately 25 ml of brandy and 10 grams (½ oz.) of sugar. Brandy is used to help quiet down the wine and stop fermentation. When pouring this brandy-sugar solution into the champagne bottle, please be gentle. Now, cork the bottles and fasten

105

these corks with specially designed wires (*see page 86*). Then, lay the bottles on their sides for another two months or possibly more, if you can stand the suspense. Check the bottles periodically. If they leak, you will notice a dark, syrupy type of solution oozing out between the top of the bottle and the place where the cork meets the bottle lip.

17. Grape Concentrates—A number of wine suppliers sell blends of concentrated grape juice to make red or white wines. These concentrates are especially attractive to the home winemaker as they are available throughout the year. A wine purist will contend that concentrates are something less than satisfactory because some of the grape's elusive character is lost in heating, evaporating, storage and shipping, but concentrates will make a very appetizing wine.

A concentrate is a juice from which much of the water has been removed. This water removal results in a syrupy solution that is about 65% sugar. Therefore, the first step is to add water. The right proportion is between three and five parts water to one part of concentrate. After adding water, the juice is handled the same as fresh-pressed juice, and it is fermented by the same method as used to ferment white wine, as there are no skins or pulp involved.

As a general rule of thumb, a net 46 fluid-ounce can of grape concentrate (which is 1 quart, 14 fluid ounces) will make 1 to 2½ gallons of white wine depending upon how much sugar and water is added. Using a 46-ounce can of 68° Brix concentrate to make a gallon will result in a sweet, heavy-bodied wine, whereas "stretching" the concentrate to make 2 or 2½ gallons will produce a light, dry wine. If you are making 1 gallon, pour the juice into the fermenter and add one can of warm water. (When using a 1-gallon container, it is not necessary to add sugar or acid-nutrient mix to start the fermentation process.) Then, attach the fermentation lock to the container and allow the juice to ferment for five days. After this period, remove the fermentation lock and add 4 cups (a standard 8-oz. measuring cup) of water to the grape concentrate. Agitate the mixture by vigorous stirring. Then replace the fermentation lock and you will note that within thirty to sixty days, the fermentation will cease as the bubbling ceases. Then siphon the clear wine into bottles that are clean and allow the wine to age.

If you have a 2-gallon or two 1-gallon containers, divide and pour the grape concentrate into the fermenting container(s). In a separate pot or pan, pour 3 cans of warm water (using the same can that contained the grape concentrate). Add 4 cups of sugar to the pan. Because the concentrate is being "stretched," it is necessary to supplement the concentrate with acid and yeast nutrient. Often, concentrate is accompanied by a packet of an "acid nutrient mix" consisting of tartaric, citric, and/or malic acids plus chemical nutrients. Add the contents of this packet to the pan. Pour this mixture into the fermenting tank(s) holding the juice concentrate and allow it to ferment for 5 days. At the end of this time, add 7 cups of water. Again, fermentation will take between 30-60 days, and then siphon the wine into bottles for aging.

If you have a 2½ gallon container, add 4 cans of warm water, 6 cups of sugar and 1 packet of the acid-nutrient mix. Then attach the fermentation lock to container. After five days remove fermentation lock, add 8 cups of water, agitate and replace fermentation lock. Allow the wine to ferment for 30-60 days and then siphon it into bottles.

SPECIAL WINE-GRAPE CONCENTRATE

The most dependable way in which the home wine-maker can produce top-quality wines time after time is with wine-grape concentrates. Good concentrates surpass in quality most of the fresh fruits or grapes that are available to the winemaker and, yet, are reasonably priced, especially in larger quantities. And, of course, using concentrates can be a year-around proposition.

There are two ways in which concentrates can be prepared. Concentrates, which normally have a natural 68% sugar content, can be reconstituted to their original state by adding 1¾ parts of water. This will produce a rather sweet, full-bodied wine. A lighter, drier wine can be made by adding additional water, sugar, yeast nutrient, and acid.

SPECIAL WINE-GRAPE CONCENTRATE

18. Vermouth—There are two kinds of Vermouth. The dry typically French Vermouth is a light, pale-colored wine that is most commonly used with gin to mix martinis. The dry Vermouth usually has a sugar percentage of 1-2%. The other type, a sweet, typically Italian type is a dark, amber-colored wine and is very commonly used as a mixture with rye or bourbon to make the well-known Manhattan.

One of the better reasons why you should consider making Vermouth is the fact that you do not have to use your better quality wines as a base, as they are not necessary. If, for example, one of your white wines has turned slightly dark due to oxidation, this wine will still make a relatively good Vermouth wine.

The first step in making Vermouth is to fortify the wine that you plan to make into Vermouth to about 18 to 22% of alcohol by volume. Then, in order to keep the wine light colored, add a neutral vodka to fortify the wine rather than a brandy as a brandy will tend to darken the wine. If the wine remains a yellowy color and you wish to lighten it, it is possible to do so by adding some activated charcoal. The correct proportion is 5 grams for every gallon of wine. To add the charcoal, draw off a little wine into a pan and then stir the charcoal and wine until it is thoroughly mixed together. The charcoal will eliminate some of the yellow color by absorbing it. Then, you should clarify the wine by filtering it. The next step is to flavor the wine by adding a very small quantity of herbs. It is possible to add an herb that is in powder form that is available from a number of wine supply dealers or it is entirely possible to make your own mixture. The correct proportion for making 4 ounces of powder is: 1 ounce of powdered genetian, 1 ounce of fennel seed, ¼ ounce of yellow blossom, dried angelica root, dried calamus root, dried camomile, and finally 1 ounce of dried and powdered balm leaf. It is also possible to add some traces of cloves, sage, dill seed, ginger, celery seed, star anise, nutmeg, cinnamon, thyme, orange and lemon rind and caraway seed. It is also possible to add spearmint, peppermint and winter-green.

To prepare the herbs, place them in a bag and soak them in water. When lowering the herbs into the water, only use enough water to cover them. Then place the herbs for a few days in the wine. The proper proportion of herbs to wine is ½ to 2 ounces of herbs to a gallon of wine.

To make sweet Vermouth, use the same methods as are used in making dry wine. First, fortify the wine with neutral vodka. Then add enough caramel syrup to make the wine light brown, chocolate colored. A small amount will do the job. Then clarify, stabilize and finish the wine by the same method that you use to make all dinner wines.

To bottle either the sweet or dry wine, use a cork or screw-cap closure and place them in storage to age.

19. Sherry—The surest method of making sherry wine is to purchase a sherry wine kit that is available from a number of wine supply dealers. A typical sherry kit will include 6 ounces of dried Muscat grapes, 1 ounce of dried bananas, 7 grams of tartaric acid, 4 grams of citric acid, 1 gram of yeast nutrient, 1 Sparkol-loid™ tablet and 1 Sherry dry wine yeast culture.

The first step is to boil the dried grapes and bananas in 1 quart of water for approximately a half hour. Allow the mixture to cool and then pour it into a fermenting container. Then pour two quarts of water into the container, add 2 pounds or approximately 4 cups of sugar and add an acid-nutrient mixture (which contains 7 grams of tartaric acid, 4 grams of citric acid and 1

111

gram yeast nutrient.) Then, vigorously shake the container to mix these ingredients together.

To begin the fermentation process, add the yeast and then cap the container with a fermentation lock. Fermentation should begin within twelve to thirty-six hours depending upon the room temperature. An ideal temperature in which to conduct fermentation is 65°-70°F. If, during the fermentation process, overflowing occurs, you should draw off some of the liquid. You will note that bubbling in the fermentation lock reaches a peak in about three days and then it will slowly start to diminish.

After allowing the mixture to ferment for approximately 3 weeks, remove the grapes and bananas by pouring the mixture through a strainer. Then, replace the fermentation lock with a wad of cloth and place the tank in a protected location outdoors where the sun will reach it. Do not disturb the juice for six months. It is quite possible that, during this six-month storage period, a "flor" or gray crust may form on the surface of the wine. This gray crust is customary when making sherry and gives sherry its special flavor. After 6 months it is time to clarify the sherry and then bottle it. To clarify, boil a Sparkolloid™ tablet in 2 ounces of water and then add this tablet to the wine. Allow three days for the wine to clear and then siphon the cleared wine into clean bottles. As an option, for a fortified sherry, add 2 ounces of vodka to each bottle prior to filling. Then cap or cork the bottle and permit it to age.

As a precaution, be sure to thoroughly clean all equipment you will be using to make sherry wine prior to using it to avoid contamination. As with all wines, if the sherry does not smell or taste good, it is possible that the wine is contaminated and should be discarded.

Part Five:

Other Fruit Wines

Any fruit or berry which can be eaten can be made into wine: apples, cherries, plums, pears, peaches, oranges, grapefruit, blackberries, elderberries, cranberries, strawberries, etc.

In selecting the fruit, be certain that it is clean, fresh and not overripe, spoiled, or moldy. The fruit also should not have served as dinner for birds or insects. If your fruit has tiny punctures or holes, there is a strong possibility your wine will turn to vinegar by bacterial contamination. We don't imagine you and your guests would enjoy this prospect.

The flavor among different fruits tends to vary considerably. Since fruits usually have strong flavors, some stronger than others, it is occasionally desirable to dilute the juice with water. The degree of dilution will depend upon your own flavor preferences. However, adding the correct amount of water is still primarily an art. You will have to decide the right amount of dilution for your tastebuds purely by experimentation. Only by trying different amounts, will you arrive at the right formulation.

We know of many hobbyists who make excellent wines from blueberries, elderberries and raspberries. The formula is 3-5 lbs. of fruit per gallon of water. Fruit wines are a lot of fun to make since they require considerable experimentation.

20. Apple Wine—Apple juice generally produces a light-bodied wine. If the acid level is right, the juice can be fermented by only adding sugar. It probably won't be necessary to adjust the acid level because most

113

apple juices are close to the ideal of .7 to 1.0% acid.

In preparing your apple juice, it may be a good idea to use several varieties of apples, including both the eating and cooking varieties. Crab apples should be included, if available, as they add astringency. When the wine is drunk, it will have a citric or persimmon-like taste sensation.

The apples can be crushed, or the juice can be extracted with an electric juicer. After the juice is extracted, it is important to add sulfite immediately (potassium or sodium bisulfite) since apple juice will oxidize quite quickly and turn brownish. Then, let the apple juice stand in the plastic fermenting container for a few hours so that the solids in the juice can drop to the container's bottom and the juice on top can be decanted, racked or siphoned into another container.

The surest method of making apple wine is to purchase pre-made, fresh apple juice, i.e., cider. (Be sure, however, to purchase cider that hasn't been treated with preservative.)

To make an apple wine that is dry and can be used as a table wine, purchase enough apples or apple juice to make 1 gallon of juice. Add 1 Campden tablet or 1 teaspoon of potassium bisulfite solution, and then add enough sugar to bring the sugar content up to 22° on the Brix scale (about 2½ cups should do the trick). Then add 1 tablespoon of strong tea that is freshly brewed or ¼ teaspoon of grape tannin powder. To start the apple juice fermenting, add 1 packet of all-purpose wine yeast.

21. Apricot Wine—It is not absolutely necessary to use fresh fruit when making apricot wine as canned or dried apricots will prove to be more than satisfactory. If the fresh apricots are hard, pour boiling water over them to soften the fruit before pulping. Pulp or liquidize according to preference and remove as many pits as possible. If you are using dried apricots, pressure cook at about 15 lbs. for approximately 5-6 minutes in ½ pint of water per pound of fruit.

To make 5 gallons of apricot wine, liquify 12 lbs. of apricots and 6 lbs. of fresh bananas in a pressure cooker. After cooking, place in a 5-gallon tank and add 2 gallons of boiled water. After cooling, add 3 gms. sodium bisulfite, 3 gms. tannin, 5 yeast nutrient and 5 pectic enzyme tablets. Measure acidity and adjust to .50%. Let the mixture rest for about 6 hours, and then strain off a sample of the juice and test for sugar. If necessary, add sugar to get to 22 to 24%.

We are now ready to add the yeast starter. If the fermentation tank is not quite full, add enough water so that only a small air space is left at the top. Stir, cover and allow it to ferment for 2 days. Open the vessel only twice a day to stir the mixture—once in the morning and once at night.

Once this step is completed, strain the contents into a new vessel. Fill as before with cool, boiled water and air-lock. Allow the contents to ferment completely and then place in a refrigerator for 3 days. Then rack. Sweeten with sugar to a specific gravity of about 1.038. As an option, you may fortify with neutral spirits so that the alcohol content is between 18-20%. Refrigerate one week and rack into a clean container. Rack again and fine as necessary. Store to mature.

The end result will be a sweet dessert wine characterized by a full flavor, body and bouquet.

22. Banana, Prune and Date Wine—To make 5 gallons of Banana-Prune-Date wine, peel and slice 12 lbs. of fresh bananas and pressure cook at 15 lbs. in a little water for about 5 minutes, or simmer for 20-30 minutes in 6 quarts of water.

Pressure cook 2 lbs. fresh prunes and 2 lbs. pitted, chopped dates for 10-15 minutes at 15 lbs. pressure in 2 quarts water, or simmer with the bananas in the 6 quarts of water. Put into a container sterilized with sodium bisulfite. Cover and let cool.

Once the mixture is cool, add 3 gms. tannin, 4½ gms. sodium bisulfite, 5 yeast nutrient and pectic enzyme tablets. Fill with enough cool, boiled water to bring the volume up to almost 5 gallons. Measure acidity and adjust to .50%. Stir and allow contents to rest for 6 hrs.

Now, strain off a sample and test for specific gravity. Adjust, if necessary, with sugar to 22 to 24%. Add yeast and allow it to ferment for 3 days. Open to stir in the morning and evening.

Strain the mixture into another sterilized 5-gallon container and fill with distilled water if necessary. Fit on an air-lock and allow the mixture to ferment. After fermentation, place in a refrigerator for 3 days. Then, rack and measure the alcoholic content. Sweeten with sugar to 1.038 and fortify to 18-20% with neutral spirits. Refrigerate one week, then rack and fine. Store until fully matured.

23. Blackcurrant Wine—To make 5 gallons of blackcurrant wine, pressure cook at 15 lbs. pressure 4½ lbs. of fresh blackcurrants, 6 lbs. of fresh bananas (peeled and sliced), and 2¼ lbs. of pitted raisins, all in a little water. Place the mixture, together with 4½ gms. sodium bisulfite, 12 gms. yeast nutrient and pectic enzyme in a sterilized container. Stir well and cover. Measure acidity and adjust accordingly to .50%. Allow it to rest for 6 hrs. and then test for sugar. Adjust to 1.100, if necessary.

Add the yeast and fill with cool, boiled water as previously noted to just under 5 gallons. Allow it to ferment for 3 days, opening only to stir morning and night. Now, strain into a fresh 5-gallon container, fill as before with cool boiled water and fit with an air-lock. Ferment until dry. Then, place in a refrigerator for 3 days. Rack and sweeten with sugar to 1.038. Finally, add 3 gms. ascorbic acid. Store, rack, and fine, accordingly. Store until you have a mature, full-bodied, unfortified dessert wine whose alcoholic content is approximately 14%.

24. Orange, Lemon and Honey Aperitif—To make 5 gallons of this wine, add the juice of 12 fresh lemons to 2 quarts of freshly squeezed orange juice in a 5-gallon, sterilized tank. To this combination, add 6 gms. sodium bisulfite immediately as well as pectic enzyme and 8 quarts of boiled water that has been allowed to cool.

Melt 8 lbs. of honey in hot water and allow it to cool before adding to the juice mixture. Put in 12 gms. yeast nutrient. Test for acidity and adjust to .7% by adding more lemon juice if acid is too low or more water if acid is too high. Measure specific gravity and adjust to 1.100.

Now, add yeast. Once the juice is fermenting well, fill the container with cool, boiled water and fit the air-lock. Ferment to dryness and refrigerate for 3 days. Rack and sweeten to taste or a specific gravity of 1.000. Add 4 gms. of ascorbic acid and 2 gms. sodium bisulfite. Rack and fine. Store to reach maturation.

Should you decide to fortify this aperitif after the first racking, do not add the closing ascorbic acid or sodium bisulfite.

25. Cherry Wine—*Selecting the fruit*—Cherry wine has a delicious flavor, particularly if a few cherry stones have been left with the juice during the fermentation process.

In selecting the cherries, choose those that are ripe for eating and have no rotten spots. Generally, 12 lbs. of cherries yield approximately 1 gallon of wine.

Preparing the fruit—To make 5 gallons of cherry wine, the first job is to wash the cherries in cold water. Then soften their skins by soaking them in boiling water. Melt 1 part of red grape concentrate in a separate pan of water. Then add 2 gms. of sodium bisulfite and set the mixture aside for about 6 hours.

During the 6-hour wait, crush the cherries after they have cooled in a crusher and remove about one half of the pits. Add about 4 gms. of sodium bisulfite, 4 pectic enzyme tablets and about 12 gms. of yeast nutrient.

The next step is to add the concentrate that you prepared 6 hours earlier. To this mixture, peel and slice 8 lbs. of bananas.. Place in a 5-gallon container and fill ¾ full with water. Stir the mixture well. Then, take a sample to check for acidity. Adjust acidity by adding tartaric acid or dilute with water to get the acid to .5%.

At the same time, check another sample for specific gravity and adjust the whole mixture by adding sugar to get to 24%, at the same time filling the container to within an inch or so of the top.

The next step is to crush and dissolve a Campden tablet and a yeast nutrient tablet and add them to the juice. At this time, stir the juice thoroughly. Cover the fermentation container and let the mixture stand overnight. The next day, add yeast and allow the container to ferment in a room with a temperature of 70°F. Allow about 4 days for this process. It is relatively important to stir or agitate the juice (must) in the container daily.

The next job is to press the mixture and transfer the juice to another container. Then, attach a water seal and permit the juice to ferment in a 70° temperature for about 5-6 days. When the fermentation starts to slow down, add 2 more cups of sugar. Stir this sugar in thoroughly and then replace the water seal and let the fermentation continue. When the fermentation is complete, place the container in a refrigerator for approximately 3 days. Then, when the wine is clear, rack or siphon it into another container. Add brandy to top off the wine. If necessary, fine with Sparkolloid™. Refrigerate the container for an additional week and then rack once more. As soon as the wine is clear, bottle it. Let the wine age for 6 months or more.

26. Elderberry Wine—There are several different types of elderberries. They can be red or white, round or oval. They can have green or red stems. They can be used fresh or dried. About 12 pounds of fresh elderberries will yield 2 gallons of wine.

In preparing the berries, use a fork to separate them from their stocks. Two possible methods of processing are: loosening the berry skins by placing them in boiling water, or by placing them in a steam juicer and extracting the wine by cooking. The latter method is undoubtedly better and easier because both the juice and skins are separated immediately. To accomplish this, you will probably have to use more than 12 pounds of elderberries in order to make your 2 gallons of wine. Separating the skin will help to prevent a bitter taste that can be caused by the skin.

If you don't have a steam juicer, crush the elderberries into a plastic fermenter which can be a standard plastic refuse container. Crush and dissolve a Campden tablet into half a glass of warm water and add pectic enzyme and yeast nutrient. Then, pour the contents of this glass into the elderberry juice. Add a gallon of very hot water to the juice and then thoroughly mix all the ingredients together. Allow this mixture to stand overnight so that it can cool. Then, add wine yeast and allow the juice to ferment under conditions of 70° to

75°F. Stir the mixture daily and, after 4 to 5 days of active fermentation, siphon or drain the juice into another container (plastic) to eliminate the pulp.

Then, add 4 cups of sugar to the juice and dissolve it into the mixture. Place a water seal on the plastic fermenting container and allow the juice to continue to ferment under a room temperature of 70° to 75°F.

When fermentation stops, rack or siphon to clear the juice.

As a finishing touch, top it off with brandy, vodka, or possibly finished elderberry, blackberry, raspberry, or strawberry wine. When the wine clears, bottle it. If additional sweetening is desired, add sugar syrup at the time you decant and serve. (Decant basically means to pour wine gently from a bottle in which sediment has deposited into a decanter or container to eliminate the sediment and make the wine clear for serving.)

27. Gooseberry Wine—*Table wine***—**Some wine connoisseurs like gooseberry wine, while others abhor it. It is pretty much a matter of individual taste. From my experience, the gooseberry can make an ideal light table wine.

Selection of gooseberries—The gooseberries must be picked or purchased in peak condition. It is possible to combine both cooking and dessert types together to make an ideal wine.

The gooseberry is an ideal fruit to extract the juice by using a fruit crusher. To make a gallon of wine, you start by using the following ingredients: 2 lbs. of sweet gooseberries and 1 lb. of green gooseberries, plus 8 ozs. of Sultana grapes. Sultana grapes are sometimes called the Thompson seedless. If you were to make a wine exclusively from these grapes, your wine would be almost completely neutral in character. This is why it makes a good combination with the gooseberry. Finally, add one-half pound of bananas.

If you don't have a pressure cooker, simmer the berries in hot water for ½ hour and then crush them into a fermentation tank. Also crush the Sultana grapes and peel and slice the bananas.

Next, add a pectic enzyme tablet. Then, add water to the juice until you have a gallon of liquid. Also, add a Campden tablet. Wait 4 hours and take both specific gravity and acidity tests. Now, add yeast and allow to ferment for 3 days. After 3 days, strain the juice into another plastic fermenter and add some more cool, boiled water. Place a water seal on the container and let the fermentation take place until the juice reaches dryness. Then, refrigerate the plastic container and add ½ gr. of sodium bisulfite (or ½ Campden tablet) and rack. Rack again if the wine does not appear clear. Then store the wine to mature.

28. Liqueurs—Cordial making can be one of the most exciting of the winemaking adventures. A number of winemaking dealers sell kits that can be used to make after-dinner cordials. These kits generally contain five bottles of essences which, when added to sugar and inexpensive Vodka or tax-paid alcohol, can make a quart of Creme de Menthe, Coffe-Moka, Cherry Brandy, Orange Brandy and Blackberry Brandy cordials.

It is also possible to obtain a Scotch-Honey Brandy from the same dealers. It is estimated that these kits will save you up to $20.

WINE INGREDIENTS KITS

Each of these four kits (Burgundy, Champagne, Rosé, and Sherry) contain all necessary ingredients (except sugar and water) to make a gallon each of very pleasant wine. They consist of various mixtures of dried Muscat or Thompson grapes, dried elderberries, yeast, yeast nutrient, and tartaric acid to make a gallon of the wine type specified. The dried fruit requires a brief cooking, but other than that, they are used much like grape concentrate. This is an ideal way to make the wine of your choice at minimal cost.

WINE INGREDIENTS KITS

Part Six:

Flower Wines

Selecting the Ingredients—Flowers offer very little help in fermentation; they do not contribute alcohol or body to the wine. Their sole function is to add flavor and bouquet. The two most popular flower wines are dandelion and rosehips, but many others are used. Remember, when gathering the flowers, that the blossoms should be picked when they are in full bloom and when the morning dew has just evaporated.

Pressing—Dandelions—The flowers are the only part of the plant that is usable. They should be simmered in water for ½ hour. As a general rule, use approximately 4 quarts of blossoms to 1 gallon of water.

Rosehips—First remove the stalk and petals from the flower and cut the remaining bud into halves. Then simmer in water for ½ hour. Approximately 12 ounces of hips should be used per gallon of water.

Flower Wines

Treating—To make 1 gallon of dandelion or rosehip wine, stir the flowers in water and bring the juice to a boil and allow to simmer for ½ hour. Allow the juice to cool. (In the case of dandelions, add 3 teaspoons of citric acid.) Then, pour the mixture of water and flowers into a 1-gallon polyethylene fermenting container and add enough additional water to fill the container ⅔ full. Add about 2 lbs. of sugar, then, after the sugar has dissolved, test for specific gravity with a hydrometer to determine if additional sugar is needed. Finally, add yeast nutrient.

Fermenting—It is not necessary to add pectic enzyme to break down pectin since pectin is not prevalent in flower petals. To begin fermentation, add yeast and allow the juice to ferment for four or five weeks. When fermentation is complete, rack several times and finally bottle. Flower wines are at their peak of excellence while still young.

Part Seven:

Wine Supplies
WINE RACKS

Wine racks come in all styles, sizes, and shapes, yet perform essentially the same task—that of storing the wine for convenient access, while allowing it to "sleep" on its side, free from vibration and in contact with its cork. From literally hundreds of different types of racks, we have carefully selected the following four, using as our criteria "beauty," "practicality," and "price."

STACKABLE 12-BOTTLE RACK

This handsome and sturdily-constructed, walnut-finished wine rack will grace any dining area and will lend appeal to wine selection. It is extremely practical, as it has built-in dowels that permit multiple stacking.

FOLDING 10-BOTTLE RACK

This finely-finished walnut rack is also extremely practical and can be folded out of the way when it is not in use. It will easily fit into cabinets or cupboards and will also make an attractive unit on a counter top or dining-room buffet.

50-BOTTLE RACK

This inexpensive rack will hold up to 50 bottles of wine in a minimum of cellar floor space. It is made with heavy-gauge steel construction and has a provision for anchoring to a wall.

"CRAMANNA" WINE CELLAR

If price is no object, this is the way to bring the wine cellar upstairs into your living area. Made by hand by expert craftsmen, this classic walnut-paneled contemporary cabinet will store up to 61 bottles of wine under perfect "cellar" temperature and humidity-controlled conditions. Operates on 110 or 220 volts A.C. current, and has a lock for safekeeping of valuable bottles.

STACKABLE 12-BOTTLE RACK

FOLDING 10-BOTTLE RACK

50-BOTTLE RACK

"CRAMANNA" WINE CELLAR

WINE BASKET

Serving red wines in a Florentine wine basket adds a bit of old world charm and a striking accent to gracious dining. This classic-designed server is made from fine willow.

SOMMELIER'S KEY AND CHAIN

Used by Sommeliers (Master Wine Stewards) throughout the world as their badge of distinction, this fine, heavy brass chain and key provides the finishing touch to your wine cellar and marks you as a Master Winemaker and wine authority. Ideal to wear at gourmet dinners and wine tastings, it is a real conversation piece and also a perfect gift.

WINE BASKET

SOMMELIER'S KEY AND CHAIN

CORKSCREWS

Drawing the cork from a wine bottle should be an act accomplished with a deft flourish—and it can be if you have a good corkscrew. The following three styles are recommended for their efficiency and simplicity.

DOUBLE-LEVER CORKSCREW

The handsomely chrome-plated corkscrew is easily operated by screwing the machine-cut "worm" into the cork and then pressing down the handles. The lever action does the job by pulling the cork up absolutely straight and unbroken.

WINE STEWARD'S CORKSCREW

The Italian corkscrew is the kind that most professional wine stewards use. It is especially good for old corks. It also operates on a leverage principle. The knife blade on the end of the corkscrew is used to cut the capsule.

RELIABLE HAND-PUMP CORK REMOVER

This cork remover is recommended by the Wine Advisory Board. It is extremely durable and is well made. To use, you push the needle through the cork and then pump the handle two or three times and out pops the cork which is clean, whole, unbroken, and there is virtually no wine spilled. It is completely safe to use and it absolutely doesn't affect the quality of the wine.

Wine Supplies

DOUBLE-LEVER CORKSCREW

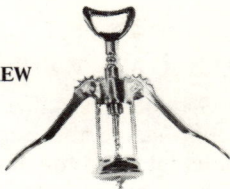

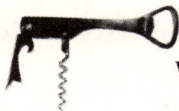

WINE STEWARD'S CORKSCREW

RELIABLE HAND-PUMP CORK REMOVER

HAND-BLOWN WINE GLASSES

The 9-ounce sparkling crystal stemware has a handsome tulip shape that serves to concentrate the aroma and bouquet and enhances the pleasure of any wine. Although they are lightweight and appear to be seemingly delicate, they are specially tempered for strength.

HAND-BLOWN CHAMPAGNE GLASSES

The graceful 5-ounce crystal tulip-shaped champagne glass will enhance any table. They are hollow stemmed and will show off the natural effervescence of sparkling wines to best advantage.

WINE BOTTLE COOLERS

Wine or champagne is served with new elegance in this unique Wine Cooler that keeps wine chilled without ice for hours. Pre-chilled wine bottle (either large or small size) is placed between refrigerating liners that contain a sealed-in, non-toxic refrigerant that retains the cold. Liners are kept in the home refrigerator freezing compartment until frozen, then placed in the cooler. Easy to care for, liners are dishwasher safe. Handsomely designed in polished black with stainless steel base, this new wine cooler is ideal for champagne, white wines, sparkling wines and aperitifs.

Wine Supplies

HAND-BLOWN WINE GLASSES

**HAND-BLOWN
CHAMPAGNE GLASSES**

WINE BOTTLE COOLERS

133

Part Eight:

Reference Tables

TABLE SHOWING AMOUNT OF JUICE (OF
KNOWN BRIX) TO BE COMBINED WITH
SUGAR TO PROVIDE A GALLON
(128 FLUID OZ.) OF MUST AT 24% SUGAR

Juice % Sugar (Brix)	Quantity of Juice in Fluid Oz.	Quantity of Sugar to Be Added	
		Av. Oz.	Cups
0%	110	35	4⅜
2	112	31	3⅞
4	113	29	3⅝
6	115	26	3¼
8	116	23	2⅞
10	118	20	2½
12	119	18	2¼
14	120	15	1⅞
16	122	12	1½
18	124	8	1
20	125	6	¾
21	125	5	⅝
22	126	3	⅜
23	127	1	⅛
24	128	0	0

SUGAR-ALCOHOL CONVERSION TABLE

Juice % Sugar (*Brix*)	*Weight of 1 Pint of Liquid in Lbs.* (*Specific Gravity*)	*Poten-tial %* *Alcohol*	*Approx. Sugar to Be Added per Gallon of Juice to Get Potential Alcohol* Up to Oz.	4% Cups	*Resulting Volume in Fluid Oz.*
0%	1.000	0%	40	5	148
1	1.004	.6	38	4¾	147
2	1.007	1.2	36	4½	146
3	1.010	1.8	34	4¼	145
4	1.014	2.4	33	4⅛	144
5	1.018	2.9	31	3⅞	143
6	1.022	3.5	29	3⅝	142
7	1.026	4.0	27	3⅜	141
8	1.030	4.6	25	3⅛	140
9	1.034	5.2	24	3	140
10	1.038	5.7	22	2¾	139
11	1.042	6.3	21	2⅝	138
12	1.046	6.9	19	2⅜	137
13	1.051	7.5	17	2⅛	137
14	1.055	8.1	16	2	136
15	1.059	8.6	14	1¾	135
16	1.063	9.1	13	1⅝	134
17	1.068	9.7	11	1⅜	134
18	1.073	10.2	9	1⅛	133
19	1.077	10.8	8	1	132
20	1.081	11.4	6	¾	131
21	1.085	12.0	5	⅝	130
22	1.089	12.7	3	⅜	130
23	1.094	13.3	1	⅛	129
24	1.099	14.0	0	0	128

APPROXIMATE* SUGAR-ALCOHOL CONTENT
DURING AND AFTER FERMENTATION

Present Specific Gravity Reading	Approx. Alcohol Content (by Vol.) for Various Specific Gravity Levels at Start of Fermentation			Approx. Sugar Content for Various Specific Gravity Levels at Start of Fermentation		
	1.08	1.09	1.10	1.08	1.09	1.10
.982	----	---	14.0%	. ---	----	0.0%
.984	—	12.5%	13.8	—	0.0%	0.4
.986	11.0%	12.3	13.6	0.0%	0.3	0.8
.988	10.7	12.1	13.3	0.3	0.7	1.2
.990	10.5	11.9	13.1	0.6	0.8	1.6
.992	10.3	11.6	12.9	0.8	1.2	2.0
.995	10.1	11.3	12.5	1.6	1.8	2.6
.997	9.9	11.0	12.2	2.0	2.2	3.0
1.000	9.6	10.7	11.9	2.8	2.9	3.6
1.002	9.3	10.5	11.7	3.1	3.3	4.0
1.005	9.0	10.1	11.3	3.8	4.0	4.7
1.010	8.4	9.5	10.7	5.0	5.1	5.7
1.015	7.8	8.9	10.1	6.0	6.1	6.8
1.020	7.2	8.3	9.5	7.1	7.2	7.8
1.030	6.0	7.1	8.3	9.3	9.3	9.8
1.040	4.8	6.0	7.1	11.5	11.5	11.8
1.050	3.6	4.8	6.0	13.6	13.6	13.9
1.060	2.4	3.6	4.8	15.7	15.7	15.9
1.070	1.2	2.4	3.6	17.9	17.8	17.9
1.080	0.0	1.2	2.4	20.0	19.9	20.0
1.090	—	0.0	1.2	—	22.0	22.0
1.100	—	—	0.0	—	—	24.0

* Because of the presence of acids and other dissolved chemicals, some of these figures may be inaccurate, particularly at the high-alcohol, low-sugar levels.

Part Nine:

Glossary

A GLOSSARY OF WINEMAKING TERMS

Every specialized activity of life has its own language. In order to more fully enjoy winemaking, it is well to become familiar with its basic vocabulary. Here, we have included various wine-tasting terms, so that you can converse freely with other winemaking hobbyists, thereby broadening your interest, understanding and enjoyment.

Acetic acid. A common organic acid best known for imparting the sour taste to vinegar. A product of microbial action, it is a major cause of spoiled wine.

Acetification. The process by which organic substances are turned into acetic acid, e.g., the making of vinegar.

Acidity. Natural and desirable acids are present in all premium-quality wines, principally tartaric acid, which imparts an agreeable tartness to fruit wines.

Aftertaste. A sensation produced in the mouth and nasal passages after swallowing which is primarily an olfactory nature.

Agar. A medium in which microorganisms may be grown, such as wine yeast.

Age. A common term which does not necessarily denote a wine's quality. Some wines are at their best after twenty or more years in the bottle. Others are at their peak after only a year's aging. An individual's own taste buds must dictate at what moment the wine is drinkable.

Aged. A term used to describe a wine having a definite bottle bouquet.

Aging. The process by which a wine matures to achieve smoothness, mellowness and unique character.

Alcohol. A common term usually used to describe ethyl alcohol, a product of microbial fermentation. In naturally fermented wine, alcohol's volumetric total is from 9 to 14 percent. In Apéritif and dessert wines, in which additional alcohol is added as pure grape spirits, it comprises between 17 and 22 percent.

Amelioration. The addition to the grape juice or new wine of any substance meant to enhance its quality; generally, the addition of water to the juice to reduce acidity.

Aperitif. A wine to which has been added a blend of herbs and spices, and which is served before a meal as a stimulant to the appetite, such as vermouths.

Appearance. The visual appeal of a wine. It is judged by overall clarity and the degree of sedimentation present which may be either colloid, that is, suspended in the liquid, or of a large particulate size settled in the bottom.

Appetizer wine. Wine that is favored and served either as a cocktail or before a meal. Favorites in this category are the sherries and vermouths, both of which may range from extra dry to semisweet.

Aroma. The natural fragrance of a wine that originates from the fermented fruit.

Aromatized wines. Either dry or sweet aperitif wines which are made by adding certain herbs or flavoring agents to the wine.

Astringency. A puckery, persimmon-like taste quality imparted to a wine by its tannin content, which is absorbed from the fruit skins and seeds. This quality will tend to lessen with bottle age.

Balance. A term used to describe a pleasant tasting wine when the many aromatic and taste substances are present in the correct proportion. A *well-balanced* wine is one in which sugar and acidity nicely complement each other.

Balling. A hydrometer or saccharometer scale graduation which gives the specific gravity of liquids. It is used to determine a wine's sugar content. This term is used interchangeably with Brix.

Bentonite. A type of clay used as a wine fining or clarifying agent.

Binning. The storing of wine in bottles for aging.

Blending. The practice of mixing, or "marrying," two or more wine products in an attempt to obtain uniform quality from year to year, or a more nearly perfect wine.

Bloom. The waxy substance covering grapes which contains natural fermentation yeasts. It is sometimes referred to as the "blush" on the grapes.

Body. The thickness or consistency of a wine. For example, a full-bodied wine, such as Burgundy, is very "winy" in taste and should be sipped. In contrast, a thin, watery wine, such as claret, is light in body and may be easily swallowed. This characteristic is occasionally referred to as "chewy."

Bond. Any alcohol beverage on which the internal revenue tax or duty has not been paid is said to be "in bond." Until the tax or duty is paid, the liquor is under government control.

Bottle. The usual U.S. wine bottle holds four-fifths of a quart, or 25.6 fluid ounces. The halves 12.8 fluid ounces. One magnum equals 2 bottles. A double magnum or jeroboam to 4 and a rehoboam to 6 bottles. European wine bottles usually contain three-fourths of a U.S. quart or 24 fluid ounces, the halves 12. European champagne comes in 26 and 13 ounce sizes.

Bottle aging. The aging of a wine while in the bottle.

Bottle fermentation. Commonly called the "true" champagne process, it is the secondary fermentation of a wine while in the bottle. It characteristically produces the wine's effervescence.

Bottle sickness. The temporary period following bottling during which the new wine is unpalatable. It generally lasts no longer than a month.

Bottoms. The sediment in a fermenter or storage container. Also called "lees."

Bouquet. The first perfume-like scent inhaled when wine is uncorked and poured. It is produced by the vaporization of esters and ethers, originating during aging. It is distinguished from aroma, the fragrance of the fruit.

Brandy. A spirit distilled from wine.

Brilliant. The quality of wine which has a sparkling clarity.

Brix. A hydrometer or saccharometer scale graduation which measures liquid specific gravity. Synonymous with balling, it is used to determine wine sugar content.

Brut. A French term applied to the driest champagnes.

Bulk process. The production of sparkling wines by secondary fermentation in vats instead of in bottles. It is also called the Charmat process.

Bung. A usually wood stopper in a keg or barrel.

Buret. A graduated, clear tube used in titration.

Burgundy. A province of France, famous for its full-bodied red wines. Also a generic name used to describe full-bodied, dry, red or white dinner wines which are strong in flavor and bouquet.

Candling. A test used to determine the clarity of a bottled wine by holding it before a light. Traditionally, a lighted candle is used.

Capsule. Coverings or closures for wine bottles used to protect the neck, to discourage refilling and to enhance visual appeal. Capsules may be made of metal foil, plastic, paper or wax.

Carbonated wines. The production of sparkling wines by injecting CO_2 into still wines.

Carbon dioxide. A common gas given off by fermentation. It is usually referred to by its chemical formula CO_2.

Carboy. A large glass bottle ranging in size from one gallon to more than 10 gallons.

Cask. A round, wooden, bulging container used for wine. Generically included in this category and by size are: puncheons, pipes, butts, hogsheads and tuns. Upright containers used for storage and fermentation are generally called vats or tanks.

Caskiness. A flavor imparted to wine by certain oils remaining in an unclean cask.

Casse. Sometimes called metal pickup, it refers to a white or colored haze caused by traces of metallic combinations in the wine. Metals often present are iron, zinc, copper and aluminum.

Cellar. Any storage place for wine either above or below ground.

Cellar treatment. The various winery processes in making wine.

Champagne. A pale gold or straw-colored sparkling dinner wine which has become effervescent by secondary fermentation. Alcoholic content ranges from 11 to 13 percent volumetrically. Other varieties are the famous pink and red champagnes usually called sparkling Burgundies.

Champagne rouge. A fermented-in-the-bottle sparkling Burgundy.

Chapeau. The thick layer or "hat" covering the must in primary fermentation.

Character. A wine possessing the proper color, bouquet, and taste that are associated with a particular genre of wine at its best.

Chateau bottled. Wine bottled at the estate or chateau at which it was grown.

Claret. Another name for Red Bordeaux wines. These dinner wines are deep red in color, tart, dry and may be either light or medium-bodied.

Clarify. The process of clearing, or "fining," cloudy wine by forcing the settlement of the minute particles.

Clean. A term that describes a wine free of any foreign flavors, and that also leaves a delightful aftertaste.

Clear. Wines that are visually clear but lack the sparkling clarity of the brilliant wines.

Clos. The enclosed or walled vineyard traditional to the old Burgundy province of France.

Cloudy. Wine marked by tiny suspended particles when disturbed or subjected to rapid temperature changes. If a wine's cloudiness does not disappear with rest, the wine is probably undrinkable.

Coarse. An unbalanced wine noted by excessive astringency, acidity or flavor intensity. A *harsh* wine is usually more unpleasant than a coarse one.

Cold Duck. A sparkling light red wine.

Colloidal Suspension. A state of liquids in which certain minute particles of semisolid remain suspended.

Color. Wines receive their color from various compounds present in the skin and flesh of the fruit. In winemaking, no artificial coloring is permitted. Colors are variegated from light straw to deep gold and from ruby to garnet.

Cooperage. A general term that designates wine containers. It was derived from the fee charged by old barrel makers or coopers for their work.

Cork. A stopper made from the spongy bark of the cork oak.

Corkscrew. A mechanical device used to remove a cork stopper.

Corky wine. A wine having an unpleasant odor due to a defect in the cork.

Cote. A French word denoting a slope on which there are vineyards.

Cradle. A device used to hold a bottle of wine at an angle and from which the wine may be poured.

Cream of tartar. Potassium acid tartrate is a white, crystalline deposit which settles out of wines during periods of low temperatures or chilling, due to decreased solubility.

Cru. The French word for growth, it denotes a vineyard of unusual quality, worthy of independent recognition under the French laws of vineyard classification.

Cuvee. A blend of new and occasionally aged wines for champagne production.

Decant. To pour clear wine gently from a bottle so as not to disturb sediment. The container into which the wine is poured is called a decanter or carafe.

Delicate. A wine with a very light flavor that can be easily destroyed when taken in mouth with full-flavored foods. Some white dinner wines are classified as delicate.

Demijohn. A large bodied, small necked wine bottle covered with wicker, holding from 1 to 5 gallons.

Demi-sec. Used to describe sparkling wines, it is a French term meaning semidry.

Dessert wine. The name of all sweet or partially sweet still wines having approximately 17 to 22 percent alcohol by volume. Examples are Port and Sherry.

Dinner wine. Wines most often served with meals. They are also called table wines, light wines, dry wines, and natural wines.

Disgorging.   Used in the making of sparkling wines, it is a process to remove sediment from bottle fermentation.

Dosage.   A sweetener added to sparkling wines before the final cork is put in the bottle.

Doux.   French for sweet, applying to sweet wine, in contrast to sec, which means dry.

Dregs.   The sediment deposited by a wine fermenting in a cask. Sometimes applied to bottle sediment.

Dry.   Lacking in sugar. A wine becomes dry once all the fermentable sugar has been converted to alcohol and carbon dioxide.

Enology.   The science and study of winemaking.

Essential oils.   Volatile oils that impart distinctive odors or flavors to plants, flowers and fruits. In wine, these oils combine with the alcohol to add to its bouquet.

Estate bottled.   Wine bottled at the estate or chateau at which it was grown, synonymous with *chateau bottled*.

Esters.   Aromatic organic chemicals formed from the chemical interaction of the wine's alcohol and acid.

Estufagems.   A winemaking process peculiar to the making of Madeira wine. In this process, the wine is initially heated in a heating chamber and warmed for approximately 6 months at a temperature of about 114 degrees F. Most Sherry wines in the U.S. are made by a similar process.

Extract.   The total solids dissolved in a wine.

Extra-dry.   Generally applied to champagne, it indicates the wine's degree of sweetness.

False wines.   Wines made with something other than grapes.

Fermentation. The chemical process whereby sugars in the presence of yeast are broken down into almost equal amounts of alcohol and carbon dioxide. This same process changes must or juice into wine.

Fermentation lock. A device which seals a container of fermenting liquor from the outside air while allowing carbon dioxide gas to escape. Also known as a water seal, water lock, or water trap.

Fermenter. The container in which juice or must is put to undergo fermentation. It is also referred to as a vat.

Fifth. The most popular American wine bottle, holding 25.6 fluid ounces, or one fifth of a gallon.

Filtering. The removal of sediment or the clarifying of wine by using filters.

Fine. To clarify a wine.

Fine wine. A mature, ideal wine which exhibits finesse.

Fining. In the cellar treatment, the process of settling the sediment.

Fino. A light, delicate, pale and usually dry Sherry.

Flat. A dull and uninteresting wine produced generally by low natural acidity and poor grape variety.

Flavored wines. Grape wines to which have been added other natural fruit or herb flavors. They may be either dry or sweet.

Flavorous. The enjoyable full flavored taste of a wine.

Flavors. Terms used to describe the complex sensations of the palate created when wine is rolled within the mouth.

Flor. The thin, white layer which appears on some Sherries during fermentation. It is produced by the flor yeast cells.

Flowers of wine. The ephemeral white skin which gradually appears on wines exposed to air.

Flowery. A wine with a bouquet that seems to smell of the actual fruit blossoms. A taste that reminds one of flowers.

Fortified wines. A wine to which spirits or brandy have been added to increase the alcoholic content.

Fortify. To increase the alcoholic content of wine to 18 percent or more by the addition of spirits or brandy.

Foxy. A unique taste which may be regarded as undesirable to some and ignored by most wine drinkers. It is a characteristic of certain old Eastern U.S. grape varieties, such as Concord grapes.

Fox grape. A common term for grapes of the species Vitus labrusca.

Free run. Juice flowing from the first light pressing of the fruit, or wine flowing freely from the residue after fermentation.

Fruit wines. Wines made from fruits other than grapes.

Fruity. The fruit-like impressions of well-made young wines caused by the high volatility of its esters. Wines that are not fruity are contrastingly called "vinous" since they are regarded as having a vine taste.

Full. A wine whose flavor, taste, or bouquet are well-balanced and pleasing.

Generic. Names that represent certain characteristics of a wine of which many are geographic in origin. For example, Burgundy, Bordeaux, Port, Sherry, Rhine Wine, and Champagne are wines that are all named after their respective viticultural districts.

Green. A term used to describe an overly acid unbalanced wine that is sometimes referred to as unripe.

Hard. A wine with extreme dryness, and more than usual acidity and excessive tannin. It is the antithesis of the soft and mellow wine, and will usually improve with age.

Harshness. The over acidity or astringency of a young wine due to its lack of maturity.

Haut. A French term denoting a wine of the Sauterne variety that is sweeter than the classic dry Sauterne.

Heady. Strong or alcoholic wines that have a generous or excessive alcoholic content.

Heavy. A wine with an increased alcoholic content but without a corresponding increase in flavor.

Hybrid. Generally, a cross between two species. Specifically, the cross between Vitis vinifera and the American species.

Hydrometer. Similar to a saccharometer, a hydrometer is an instrument used for measuring the density of liquids.

Keg. A small cask.

Kniffin. A method of training grape vines.

Lees. The sediment or dregs deposited by wine during fermentation and aging which consists primarily of tartrate and spent yeast.

Light. A quality of a pleasing, dry, and refreshing wine.

Mature. A term used to describe a wine possessing a balanced, aged bouquet and one which is ready for bottling and/or drinking.

Mellow. A word which describes a soft, sometimes slightly sweet wine.

Moldy. An odor resulting from using moldy grapes or moldy cooperages.

Must. Unfermented grape juice and pulp in the process of becoming wine.

Musty. A wine having the odor of damp, decaying wood. Sometimes called mousy wine, this product should be discarded.

Natural Fermentation. Fermentation initiated under normal factors, producing an alcoholic strength consistent with the degree of natural microbial action that can be expected from already present juice sugars.

Natural wines. Wines produced through natural fermentation in contrast to fortified wines.

Noble rot. A fungus which develops on the skins of ripe grapes in well-defined geographical sectors. This fungus penetrates the grape skin without breaking it, resulting in a grape that begins to wither without spoiling, thereby concentrating the juice. Grapes having the "noble rot" will have a very high sugar content. Examples of wines made from such grapes are the German Auslese wine and the Tokay wine of Hungary.

Nose. A professional wine taster's term describing bouquet. For example, a wine with a good nose has a good bouquet.

Nutty. A word used to describe the preferable, nut-like flavor of certain appetizer and dessert wines. The Spanish call this pungent flavor "rancio."

Odor. The smell of a wine.

Off-odor. Any odor which is foreign to the normal smell of a sound wine.

Oxidation. A chemical change initiated by wine coming in contact with oxygen. This change may be either advantageous or disadvantageous. For instance, oxidized white wine will generally turn an unappealing tan or brown.

Parts per million. A chemical term abbreviated ppm that is used to denote small quantities, for example, one pound of sugar in a million pounds of water.

Pasteurization. The process of heating liquids for a period of time to a temperature of 140 to 180 degrees Fahrenheit to arrest microbial action. In winemaking, it is sometimes used to stop fermentation.

Perfume. A wine's bouquet.

Petillant. Also called "crackling wine," it describes a wine having a slight content of carbon dioxide.

Glossary

Piquant. French for just the right amount of acidity. Generally applied to white dinner wines.

Pomace. The crushed skin, pulp and seeds that remain after the pressing of the fruit. Also called marc.

Pop wines. Wines with artificial flavors, such as "Strawberry Hill," "Cinnamon," "Apple," "Zapple," and "Love."

Port. A deep red dessert wine which is very sweet and full-bodied.

Press. A device which forces juice from the fruit by applied direct pressure.

Proof. A system used for measuring alcoholic strength which is rarely used for wine. Approximately one percent by volume equals two degrees of proof.

Racking. The pumping out, siphoning or drawing off of wine from its lees into a fresh storage container.

Red dinner wines. Rich dry wines that are occasionally tart and astringent. They are usually served with red meats and highly seasoned foods.

Reducing sugar. A complex sugar, such as sucrose, is inverted by the action of invertase, a yeast enzyme, into the sugars, glucose (also called Dextrose) and fructose. Therefore, table sugar, when added to juices or wine, will not have its presence immediately detected. Resultant reducing sugars, inverted by chemical action, are only tested for by today's winemaking kits.

Rhine wine. Generically named, these wines were originally produced in Germany. They are light, dry, and tart white dinner wines varying from pale gold to a slight greenish hue. They are similar to the Hock and Riesling wines.

Rich. A full-bodied, flavorful wine. Also called robust or generous.

Riddling. The procedure during traditional champagne-making by which sediment is worked into the neck of the bottle.

Ripe. A wine at its mellowest and attainable best. The term "ripe for bottling" denotes that the wine has improved as far as possible in vat storage after which aging is completed in the bottle.

Ropiness. A fault of wine typified by viscosity due to a lack of astringent matter, principally tannic acid.

Rosé. A pink dinner wine that is fruity, ranging in taste from dry to slightly sweet. It is generally used during luncheon or as an all-occasion wine.

Rounded. A wine in which body and flavor are united harmoniously.

Saccharometer. A graduated scale for a hydrometer used to read the specific gravity of liquids or their sugar contents. This instrument is also called a mustimeter.

Sauterne. A full-bodied, golden-hued, white dinner wine that ranges from dry to sweet but that is generally semi-sweet.

Scud. Easily recognized as particles that dart about at the slightest movement of the bottle, this mold attacks white wines deficient in alcohol.

Sec. A French word for dry.

Sediment. The solid matter precipitated by a wine during fermentation and aging. It is generally more pronounced in the red wines than the white ones.

Sekt. A German word for sparkling wine.

Sherry. A generic name originating from Spain, this wine has a characteristic nutty flavor. This flavor is imparted by aging at a warm temperature through flor yeast fermentation. Sherry may range in color from pale to dark amber, and either dry, medium-dry, or sweet. The sweet is usually called "Cream Sherry." In the U.S., these wines are not produced by traditional methods.

Siphon. A device, principally consisting of a hose, by

which liquids may be transferred to a container at a lower level over an intermediate elevation.

Soft.   A well-balanced wine low in astringency, synonymous with smooth.

Solera.   A Spanish system of blending and maturing wines, especially dessert wines. It consists of using a series of casks graduated by age. Young wines are constantly refreshed with older ones to sustain the same wine quality over the years.

Sour.   A disagreeable taste caused by excessive acetic acid. A "sour wine" is a spoiled one. Do not confuse this wine with a dry, astringent or tart one.

Sparkling Burgundy.   Red Burgundy wine made to effervesce either by bulk processing or the champagne method.

Sparkling wines.   These are wines in which the carbon dioxide accumulated during the second fermentation is absorbed in the wine while either in the bottle (true champagne process) or within a closed vat (bulk process). Subsequently, these wines effervesce on being opened. Champagne and Sparkling Burgundy are examples.

Spatlese.   Traditionally from Germany and Hungary, these wines are produced by leaving the grapes on the vine long past ripening and are naturally sweet.

Spicy.   A pleasing, piquant flavor often experienced in white dinner wines.

Spigot.   A faucet, usually wood, that is used to draw off the contents of a cask.

Split.   A small bottle holding either 6.4 or 8 fluid ounces used generally for champagne.

Still wines.   Non-sparkling table wines in which the CO_2 gas formed in fermentation has been allowed to escape. These wines are usually less than 14 percent alcohol.

Stuck wine. A wine that has ceased fermentation before all the sugar has been changed to alcohol.

Sulfiting. The addition to must of potassium or sodium metabisulfite.

Sulfur dioxide. Symbolized SO_2. Sulfur is added to wine to kill deleterious yeast, fungi, and bacteria. However, caution must be exercised since the desirable Saccharomyces yeasts may also be killed by too high a concentration of sulfur.

Sweetness. The sensation of taste derived mainly from the presence of sugars, specifically, glucose and fructose. Glycerol also contributes to a sweet taste. In wines, sweetness is counteracted by acidity and astringency.

Syphon. See siphon.

Tannic acid. Derived from grape skins, stems and pips, this astringent acid is essential to properly mature and keep the wine. It is the same as tannin.

Tannin. This substance imparts a puckery taste sensation to wine. See tannic acid.

Tart. Wines having an agreeable fruit-acid flavor. Sometimes described as being crisp, these wines offer a pleasing freshness and balance with high acidity.

Tartaric acid. The most important fixed acid found in wine. In its purified form, it is known as cream of tartar.

Taste. There are 4 classes of true taste sensations: sour or acid, sweet, bitter or salt. The tactile ability to distinguish viscosity also is of importance. In tasting wines, however, there are a number of other sensations due to the complex interactions of both taste and olfactory receptors. For this reason, the taste of wine is classified according to acidity, sweetness, body, astringency and flavor.

Glossary

Tawny.   A brownish-red color in red wines aged for a long period of time. Especially refers to tawny Port.

Varietal wine.   A wine named after the principal grape variety which it contains. Regulations require that at least 51 percent of a varietal wine by volume be derived from its particular grape in addition to its characteristic flavor and aroma.

Vermouth.   A white or red, dry or sweet wine flavored with various combinations of herbs and other aromatic substances.

Vin gris.   A French term for a pink wine that is ofttimes produced from grapes having a pink juice. These grapes may be found in the province of Lorraine.

Vinification.   The conversion of grape juice into wine.

Vin ordinaire.   French for common wine.

Vinosity.   The "winy" quality of wines made from grapes. It is derived from the combination of flavor, bouquet, and body.

Vintage.   The harvesting, crushing or fermenting of grapes into wine. Also, the crop of grapes in a certain year. A vintage wine is one that is labeled with the year of the crop marked on the label. A vintage year is one in which the grapes reach full maturity and the wine made from them is of especially good quality.

Vintner.   Generally, anyone associated with the making or marketing of wine. Specifically, the winemaker.

Viscidity.   A fault of wine which causes it to become viscuous due to a lack of astringent matter, particularly tannin.

Viticulture.   The science or study of vine production; also, the cultivation of the vine. Sometimes called viniculture when applied to the growing of grapes for wine.

Volatile oil.   Any oil that readily vaporizes.

White dinner wines.   Ranging from pale straw to deep gold in color, these delicate wines vary from extremely dry and tart to sweet and full-bodied. They are best served with white meats, fowl and seafoods.

Wine.   Specifically, the fermented juice of fresh ripe grapes, used as a beverage, in cooking, and in various religious rites.

Winegrowing.   The entire process of growing the fruit on the vine, fermenting it and making the wine. The producer is called the winegrower, or winemaker.

Winery.   A building or room in which juice is fermented into wine.

Woody.   A wood-like flavor imparted to old wines by aging for a long period in wooden cooperage.

Yeasts.   Microorganisms used by modern wineries to start fermentation. Wild yeasts, found on grapes, may spontaneously initiate fermentation themselves. However, not all types of yeasts are desirable.

Yeasty.   Wines that either taste or smell of yeast.

FEDERAL REGULATIONS

Repeal of the 18th Amendment in 1933 again made home winemaking legal up to 200 gallons per year for the personal consumption of the family. While this is a generous allowance, the law is rather specific. It states that the maker of wine must be the head of the household, that the wine can be used only for home consumption, and that it cannot be offered for sale.

The only requirements that the government places on winemakers are that they register their winemaking activities by filling out Form No. 1541 and sending it to the Alcohol Tax Unit of the local Bureau of Internal Revenue, and that the winemaker keep a record of his production. Copies of Form No. 1541 may be obtained from the following Alcohol Tax Units:

55 TREMONT ST.
BOSTON, MASS. 02148

17 NO. DEARBORN ST.
CHICAGO, ILL. 60602

275 PEACHTREE ST. N.E.
ATLANTA, GA. 30303

1114 COMMERCE ST.
DALLAS, TEXAS 75202

215 N. 17TH ST.
OMAHA, NEBR. 68102

2 PENN CENTER PLAZA
PHILADELPHIA, PA 19102

90 CHURCH ST.
NEW YORK, N.Y. 10007

222 EAST CENTRAL PKWY.
CINCINNATI, OHIO 45202

870 MARKET STREET
SAN FRANCISCO, CAL. 94104

Wine Log

NAME OF WINE .... No. ....

Gallons .... Date Started ....

	Type	*Quantity*	*Preparation*
Ingredients 1	....	....	....
Ingredients 2	....		
Ingredients 3	....		

Initial Acidity of Juice .... Acid Added .... or

Water Added .... or Calcium Carbonate Added ....

Final Acidity of Juice ....

Brix Before Sugar Added ....

Quantity of Sugar Added ....

Brix After Sugar Added ....

Yeast Type Added .... Date ....

Sterilizer Added ....

Yeast Nutrient Added ....

Date Fermentation Ended .... Specific Gravity ....

For Sparkling Wine Only:

Additional Sugar Added ....

Additional Water Added ....

Date ....

Fining and Racking

	Agent	Date Added	Date of Racking	Appearance
1.				
2.				
3.				

Date Sealed for Storage ⸺⸺⸺⸺⸺

Date to Be Opened (Tank) ⸺⸺⸺⸺

Date Bottled ⸺⸺⸺⸺⸺⸺⸺

Date to Be Opened (Bottles) ⸺⸺⸺

Appreciation

Bouquet ⸺⸺⸺⸺ Flavor ⸺⸺⸺⸺

Body ⸺⸺⸺⸺⸺ Color ⸺⸺⸺⸺

Alcohol % ⸺⸺⸺ Acid % ⸺⸺⸺

Dry ☐   Medium ☐   Sweet ☐

Method Used in Production

Comments

Wine Log

NAME OF WINE .... No. ....

Gallons .... Date Started ....

	Type	Quantity	Preparation
Ingredients 1	....	....	....
Ingredients 2	....	....	....
Ingredients 3	....	....	....

Initial Acidity of Juice .... Acid Added .... or

Water Added .... or Calcium Carbonate Added ....

Final Acidity of Juice ....

Brix Before Sugar Added ....

Quantity of Sugar Added ....

Brix After Sugar Added ....

Yeast Type Added .... Date ....

Sterilizer Added ....

Yeast Nutrient Added ....

Date Fermentation Ended .... Specific Gravity ....

For Sparkling Wine Only:

Additional Sugar Added ....

Additional Water Added ....

Date ....

158

Fining and Racking

	Agent	Date Added	Date of Racking	Appearance
1.				
2.				
3.				

Date Sealed for Storage _____

Date to Be Opened (Tank) _____

Date Bottled _____

Date to Be Opened (Bottles) _____

Appreciation

Bouquet _____ Flavor _____

Body _____ Color _____

Alcohol % _____ Acid % _____

Dry ☐   Medium ☐   Sweet ☐

Method Used in Production

Comments